Access
Made Simple

Made Simple *Computer Books*

● **easy to follow**   ● **jargon free**   ● **practical**   ● **task based**   ● **easy steps**

Thousands of people have already discovered that the **MADE SIMPLE** series gives them what they want *fast!* These are the books for you if you want to **learn quickly what's essential** and **how** to do things with a particular piece of software. You are:

● **a Secretary** or **temp** who wants to **get the job done**, **quickly** and **efficiently**

● **a Manager**, without the time to learn all about the software but who wants to **produce** **letters, memos, reports** or **spreadsheets**

● someone **working from home**, who needs a **self-teaching** approach, that gives **results fast**, with the least confusion.

For **clarity** and **simplicity**, the **MADE SIMPLE** Computer Books stand above all others.

This **best selling** series is in your **local bookshop now**, or in case of difficulty, contact:

Reed Book Services Ltd., Orders Dept, PO Box 5, Rushden, Northants, NN10 9YX. Tel 0933 58521. Fax 0933 50284. Credit card sales 0933 410511.

Series titles:

AmiPro for Windows	Moira Stephen	0 7506 2067 6	
Excel for Windows	Stephen Morris	0 7506 2070 6	
Lotus 1-2-3 (DOS)	Ian Robertson	0 7506 2066 8	
MS-DOS	Ian Sinclair	0 7506 2069 2	
MS-Works for Windows	P. K. McBride	0 7506 2065 X	
Windows 3.1	P. K. McBride	0 7506 2072 2	
Word for Windows	Keith Brindley	0 7506 2071 4	
WordPerfect (DOS)	Stephen Copestake	0 7506 2068 4	
Access for Windows	Moira Stephen	0 7506 2309 8	*NEW!
The Internet	P.K.McBride	0 7506 2311 X	*NEW!
Quicken for Windows	Stephen Copestake	0 7506 2308 X	*NEW!
WordPerfect for Windows	Keith Brindley	0 7506 2310 1	*NEW!
Lotus 123 (5.0) for Windows	Stephen Morris	0 7506 2307 1	June '95
Multimedia	Simon Collin	0 7506 2314 4	June '95
Pageplus for Windows	Ian Sinclair	0 7506 2312 8	June '95
Powerpoint	Moira Stephen	0 7506 2420 5	June '95
Harddisk Management	Ian Sinclair	0 7506 2421 3	October '95
Windows 95	P.K. McBride	0 7506 2306 3	October '95

Access
Made Simple

Moira Stephen

Made Simple
BOOKS

Made Simple
An imprint of Butterworth-Heinemann Ltd
Linacre House, Jordan Hill, Oxford OX2 8DP

ℛ   A member of the Reed Elsevier plc group

OXFORD   LONDON   BOSTON
MUNICH   NEW DELHI   SINGAPORE   SYDNEY
TOKYO   TORONTO   WELLINGTON

First published 1995
© Moira Stephen 1995

TRADEMARKS/REGISTERED TRADEMARKS
Computer hardware and software brand names mentioned in this book are protected
by their respective trademarks and are acknowledged.

British Library Cataloguing in Publication Data
A catalogue record for this book is available from the British Library

ISBN 0 7506 2309 8

⌂ Design and Typeset by P.K.McBride, Southampton

Archetype, Bash Casual, Cotswold and Gravity fonts from Advanced Graphics Ltd
Icons designed by Sarah Ward © 1994
Printed and bound in Great Britain by Scotprint, Musselburgh, Scotland

Contents

Preface

The computer is about as simple as a spacecraft, and who ever let an untrained spaceman loose? You pick up a manual that weighs more than your birth-weight, open it and find that its written in computerspeak. You see messages on the screen that look like code and the thing even makes noises. No wonder that you feel it's your lucky day if everything goes right. What do you do if everything goes wrong? Give up.

Training helps. Being able to type helps. Experience helps. This book helps, by providing training and assisting with experience. It can't help you if you always manage to hit the wrong keys, but it can tell you which are the right ones and what to do when you hit the wrong ones. After some time, even the dreaded manual will start to make sense, just because you know what the writers are wittering on about.

Computing is not black magic. You don't need luck or charms, just a bit of understanding. The problem is that the programs that are used nowadays look simple but aren't. Most of them are crammed with features you don't need – but how do you know what you don't need? This book shows you what is essential and guides you through it. You will know how to make an action work and why. The less essential bits can wait – and once you start to use a program with confidence you can tackle these bits for yourself.

The writers of this series have all been through it. We know your time is valuable, and you don't want to waste it. You don't buy books on computer subjects to read jokes or be told that you are a dummy. You want to find what you need and be shown how to achieve it. Here, at last, you can.

1 Getting started

What is a database?

A **database** is simply a collection of data. It may be an address list, employee details or details of items in stock.

Access is a **relational** database - this means that all related data is stored in one place. If you are storing data about your business, you could have your employee data, customer data, product data, supplier data etc all stored in your Company Database.

Table

In a relational database, all the data on one topic is stored in a **table**. You would have a table for your employee data, a table for your customer data, a table for your product data etc. If your database requirements are fairly simple, you might have only one table in your database. If your requirements are more complex, your database may contain several tables.

The data in the table is structured in a way that will allow you to interrogate the data when and as required. All of the data on one item, eg an employee or a stock item, is held in the record for that employee or stock item, within the appropriate table.

Record

A **record** contains information about a single item in your table. All the detail relating to one employee will be held in that employee's record. All the detail on a customer will be held in a record for that customer. The detail is broken down into several fields – one for each piece of detail about your item (employee, stock item, etc).

Exam Table ~~class~~ ~~Super~~
Disabled Table

COMPANY DATABASE FILE

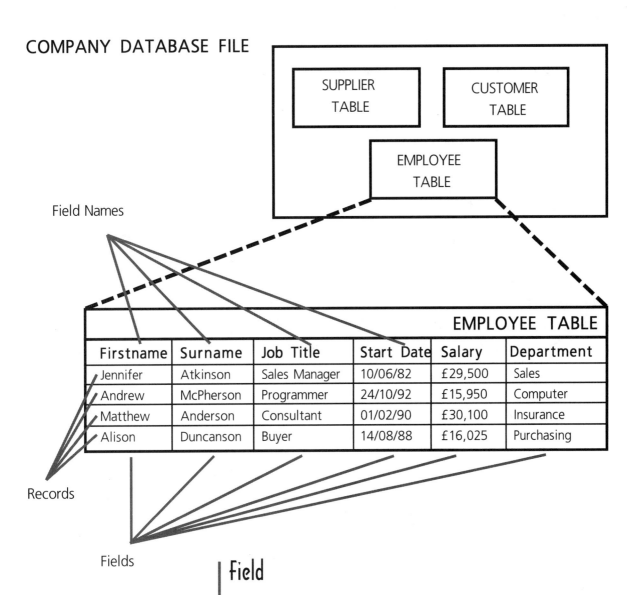

Field Names

SUPPLIER TABLE

CUSTOMER TABLE

EMPLOYEE TABLE

EMPLOYEE TABLE

Firstname	Surname	Job Title	Start Date	Salary	Department
Jennifer	Atkinson	Sales Manager	10/06/82	£29,500	Sales
Andrew	McPherson	Programmer	24/10/92	£15,950	Computer
Matthew	Anderson	Consultant	01/02/90	£30,100	Insurance
Alison	Duncanson	Buyer	14/08/88	£16,025	Purchasing

Records

Fields

Field

A **field** is a piece of data within a record. In an employee's record things like firstname, surname, job title, address, age, salary etc would all be held in separate fields. In a stock item record, you would have fields for stock number, description, price etc.

Each field has a name that identifies it.

Access objects

When working in Access, you find six different types of **objects** that are used to input, display, interrogate, print and automate your work. These objects are listed in the Database Window.

Tables

Tables are the most important object in your database. Tables are used for data entry, viewing data and displaying the results of queries. (*See sections 3-7*)

Table

In a Table each record is displayed as a **row** and each field is displayed as a **column**. You can display a number of records on the screen at any one time, and as many fields as will fit on your screen. Any records or fields not displayed can be scrolled into view as required.

Queries

You use **queries** to locate specific records within your tables. You might want to extract records that meet specific selection criteria (eg all employees on Grade G in the Accounts department). When you run a Query, the results are displayed in a Table. (*See section 8*)

Query

Forms

You can use **forms** to provide an alternative to tables for data entry and viewing records. With forms, you arrange the fields as required on the screen - you can design your forms to look like the printed forms (invoices, order forms etc) that you use.

Form

When you use forms, you display one record at a time on your screen. (*See section 9*)

Report

Macro

Module

Reports

Reports can be used to produce various printed outputs from data in your database.

Using reports, the same database can produce a list of customers in a certain area, a set of mailing labels for your letters, or a report on how much each customer owes you. (*See section 10*)

Macros & Modules

Macros and **modules** are used to automate the way you use Access, and can be used to build some very sophisticated applications.

They are well beyond the scope of a Made Simple book!

Tip

Learn to recognise these icons — they can speed up your work.

Preparing your data

The most important (and often difficult) stage in setting up your database takes place away from the computer. Before you set up a database you must get your data organised. You must ask yourself two key questions

- What information do I want to store?

- What do I want to get out of my database?

NB You must also work out your answers to these two questions!?!

Once you've decided what you are storing, and what use you intend to make of the data, you are ready to start designing your database. Again, much of this can be done away from the computer.

What fields do you need?

You must break the data down into the smallest units you will want to search or sort on. Each of these must be a separate field.

If you are setting up **names**, you would probably break the name into three fields - *Title*, *Forenames* (or initials) and *Surname*. This way you can sort the file into Surname order, or search for someone using the Forename and Surname.

If you are storing **addresses**, you would probably want separate fields for *Town/city*, *Region* and/or *Country*. You can then sort your records on any of these fields, or locate records by specifying appropriate search criteria. For example, using Town/city and Country fields, you could search for addresses in Perth (*Town/city*), Australia (*Country*) rather than Perth (*Town/city*), Scotland (*Country*).

Tip

When planning your database, take a small sample of the data to be stored and examine it carefully. Break each item into its smallest units (fields). You can then work out what fields you will need to be able to store all the necessary data for all the items.

How big are the fields?

You must also decide how much space is required for each field. The space you allocate must be long enough to accommodate the longest item that might go there. How long is the longest surname you want to store? If in doubt, take a sample of some typical names (McDonald, Peterson, MacKenzie, Harvey-Jones?) and add a few more characters to the longest one to be sure. An error in field size isn't as serious as an error in record structure, as field sizes can be expanded without existing data being affected.

It is *very important* that you spend time organising and structuring your data *before* you start to computerise it - it'll save you a lot of time and frustration in the long run!

Take note

Spend time ORGANISING your data before you start. Decide WHAT you want to store, and WHAT you want to do with it. Work out what FIELDS are required (for sorting and searching).

You can edit the structure of your table if necessary - but hunting through existing data to update records is time consuming, so it's best to get it right to start with!

Getting into Access

Basic steps

It is assumed that Access is already installed on your computer. If it isn't, you must install it (or get someone else to install it for you) before going any further.

If necessary, switch on your PC and go into Windows.

If you've been using another Windows applications, save any files you want to keep, close the applications you've been using, and go back to the Program Manager window.

You're now ready to start using Access.

1 At the **Program Manager** window, open the group (probably **Microsoft Office**) that has Access in it, by double clicking its icon.

2 Double click the **Access** icon to start the package running.

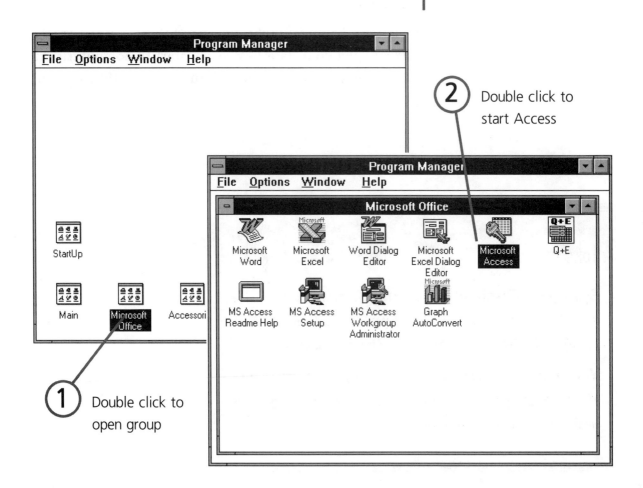

② Double click to start Access

① Double click to open group

8

Cue cards

3 If this is the first time you've used Access, a Cue Card will appear on the screen. Select the " **Don't display this startup card again**" checkbox.

4 Close the Cue Card by double clicking its Control Menu button.

5 You should now see the Access screen.

You can get an introduction to Access by selecting any topic listed on the Cue Card. To choose one of the topics listed, click on the button to the left to the topic.

I suggest you leave the Cue Cards for the time being and look at them later.

Take note

If you've already been into Access, and selected the "Don't display this startup card again" checkbox, you jump from Step 2 to Step 5 - the Access screen.

---

④ Double click to close

③ Check if you don't want this again

MS Access Cue Cards

| Menu | Search | Back |

🔑 Welcome to Microsoft Access 2.0

▶ Here are some ways you can get started:

> **Get a quick introduction** and overview of Microsoft Access in Cue Cards. See what a Microsoft Access database is and what you can do with it.

> **Explore a sample database** using Cue Cards. Open the Northwind Traders database and learn about Microsoft Access by working with data in the database.

> **Create a new database** using Cue Cards, a friendly online coach that walks you through the steps and teaches you about Microsoft Access as you do your own work.

> Read **Getting Started**, a printed tutorial that uses real-life examples to show you how to create and use a Microsoft Access database.

> **Start the Solutions sample application** to see commonly used forms, reports, and other application features, along with step-by-step instructions on how to create them.

> Read **Help** to find out what's new in Microsoft Access version 2.0.

☒ Don't display this startup card again.

The Access screen

Looking at the Access screen, you can identify the standard elements of any Window.

The Title Bar, Menu Bar and Toolbar; the Minimise, Maximise/Restore and Control Menu Buttons; and the Status Bar.

I suggest you Maximise the Access application window. This way you won't be distracted by other windows that may be open on your desktop.

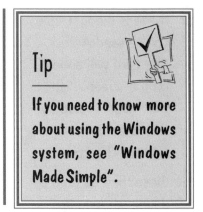

Tip

If you need to know more about using the Windows system, see "Windows Made Simple".

Control Menu
Button

Menu Bar

Title Bar

Toolbar

Minimize

Maximize/
Restore

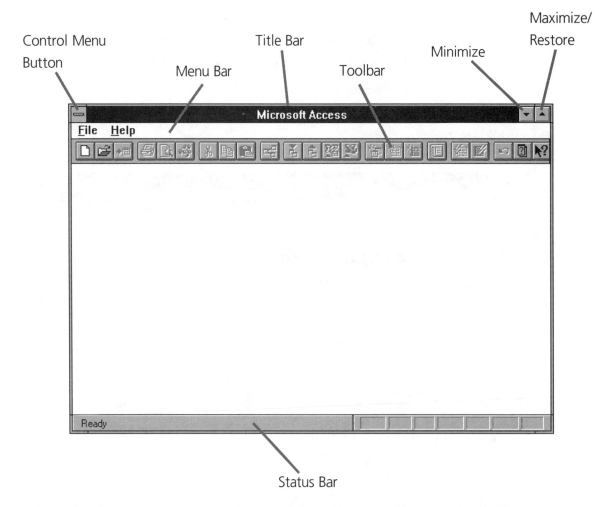

Status Bar

Basic Steps

Exiting Access

1 Double click the **Control Menu Button** on the **Title Bar**

or

1 Open the **File** Menu

2 Choose **Exit**

When you have completed your session in Access, you must exit the package and return to the Windows environment (*don't* just switch off your computer!!). To exit the package, use one of the methods suggested.

(1) Open the File menu

(1) Double click

```
─                    Microsoft Access                    ▼ ▲
 File  Help
 [toolbar icons]
```

```
File
    New Database...            Ctrl+N
    Open Database...           Ctrl+O
    Compact Database...
    Convert Database...
    Encrypt/Decrypt Database...
    Repair Database...

    Toolbars...
    Unhide...
    Run Macro...
    Add-ins                         ▶

    1 DB1.MDB
    2 DB2.MDB
    3 SAMPAPPS\NWIND.MDB

    Exit
```

Ready

(2) Choose Exit

Summary

- A **database** is a collection of data

- Access is a **relational** database

- In a relational database, all related data is stored in one place

- A relational database is organised into **tables**, **records** and **fields**

- In Access, you will encounter various database objects - **tables**, **queries**, **forms**, **reports**, **macros** and **modules**

- **Preparation** is the first, very important, step in setting up your database

- To **get into Access**, open the Microsoft Office group, then double click the Access application icon

- To **get out of Access**, double click the Control Menu button on the Application window, or choose Exit from the File menu

2 Help

Browsing

When working in the Windows environment there is always plenty of help available - in books, in manuals, in magazines and on-line. The trick is being able to find the help you need, when you need it. In this section, we look at the various ways you can interrogate the on-line Help when you discover you're in need of it.

There are several ways you can dip into Help, and you can choose the most suitable method, depending on what you are doing. You can:-

● Browse through the on-line Help to get a feel for what is there as described here, or

● Search for help on a specific topic once you know what you need help on

● Use Context Sensitive Help to get help with Menu items and Dialog boxes

● View Cue cards to help you work through new tasks

1 Open the **Help** Menu

2 Choose **Contents**

3 From the **Contents** window, click on the green underlined topic that interests you, eg *"Using Microsoft Access"*

4 From the list of options displayed, click on the topic with the green underline that you are interested in eg *" Forms "*. Continue until you have found the help page that has the information you want to read

5 Double click the Control Menu button on the Help Window to close Help

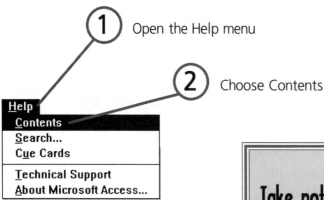

① Open the Help menu

② Choose Contents

| Help |
| Contents |
| Search... |
| Cue Cards |
| Technical Support |
| About Microsoft Access... |

Take note

If you choose an item with a dotted green underline, a definition of that item is displayed. To close the definition box, click anywhere outside it.

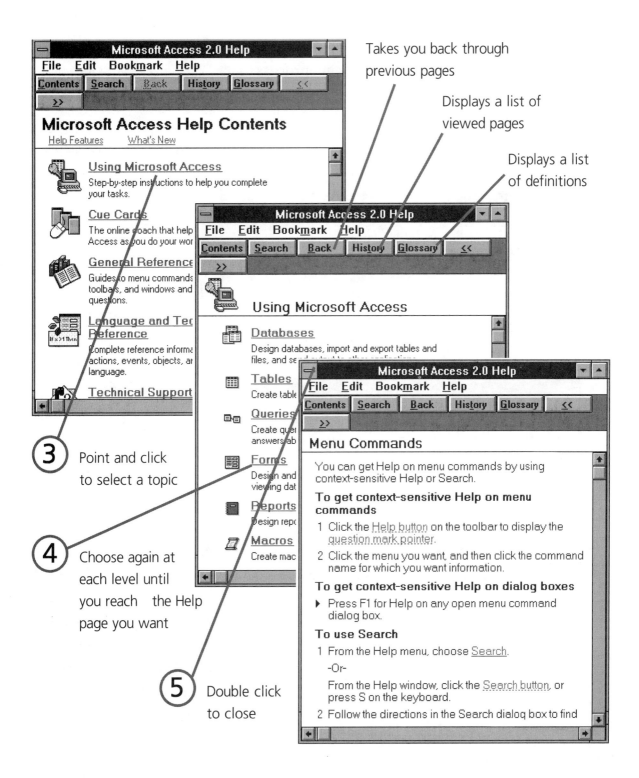

Takes you back through
previous pages

Displays a list of
viewed pages

Displays a list
of definitions

Microsoft Access 2.0 Help

File   Edit   Bookmark   Help

Contents | Search | Back | History | Glossary | << |
>> |

Microsoft Access Help Contents

Help Features   What's New

Using Microsoft Access
Step-by-step instructions to help you complete
your tasks.

Cue Cards
The online coach that help
Access as you do your wor

General Reference
Guides to menu commands
toolbars, and windows and
questions.

**Language and Tec
Reference**
Complete reference informa
actions, events, objects, an
language.

Technical Support

Microsoft Access 2.0 Help

File   Edit   Bookmark   Help

Contents | Search | Back | History | Glossary | << |
>> |

Using Microsoft Access

Databases
Design databases, import and export tables and
files, and se

Tables
Create table

Queries
Create quer
answers ab

Forms
Design and
viewing dat

Reports
Design repo

Macros
Create mac

Microsoft Access 2.0 Help

File   Edit   Bookmark   Help

Contents | Search | Back | History | Glossary | << |
>> |

Menu Commands

You can get Help on menu commands by using
context-sensitive Help or Search.

**To get context-sensitive Help on menu
commands**

1 Click the Help button on the toolbar to display the
question mark pointer.

2 Click the menu you want, and then click the command
name for which you want information.

To get context-sensitive Help on dialog boxes

▶ Press F1 for Help on any open menu command
dialog box.

To use Search

1 From the Help menu, choose Search.
-Or-
From the Help window, click the Search button, or
press S on the keyboard.

2 Follow the directions in the Search dialog box to find

③ Point and click
to select a topic

④ Choose again at
each level until
you reach   the Help
page you want

⑤ Double click
to close

Search

Browsing as described above, although interesting when you have the time, can be a time-consuming process.

If you know *what* you need help on, you will probably be quicker **Searching** for the topic.

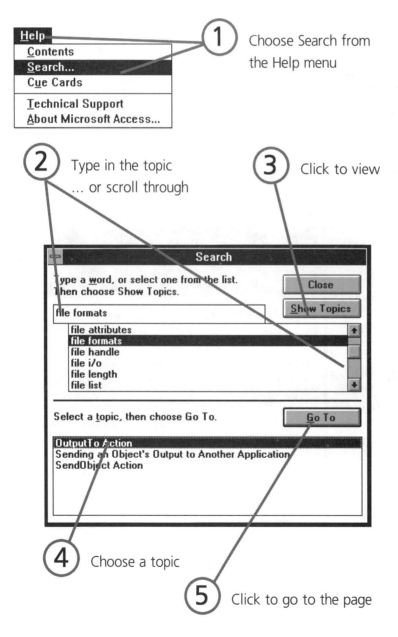

Choose Search from the Help menu

② Type in the topic ... or scroll through

③ Click to view

④ Choose a topic

⑤ Click to go to the page

1 Open the **Help** menu and choose **Search**

2 Start typing in the name of the topic you want help on (or scroll through the list until you see it)

3 Choose **Show Topics** to display those related to the chosen item

4 Select the item that interests you from the list

5 Click **Go To** to display the page for this topic

6 Double click the **Control Menu** button on the Help window to close Help when you're finished

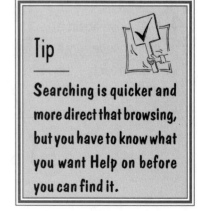

Tip

Searching is quicker and more direct that browsing, but you have to know what you want Help on before you can find it.

Basic steps

❑ **Help on the Tools or Menu Items**

1 Click the **Help** icon

either

2 Click on the **tool** that interests you - this displays Help on the selected tool

or

2 Click on the **menu** that interests you

3 Click on the **menu item** that you want Help on - you are taken directly to its Help Page

Context sensitive Help

Context sensitive Help is a very direct way of getting help on whatever you are working on. There are 2 main methods here -

● Help on the the Tools or Menu Items

● Help on the Dialog Boxes

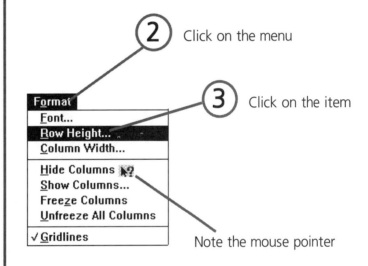

② Click on the menu

③ Click on the item

Note the mouse pointer

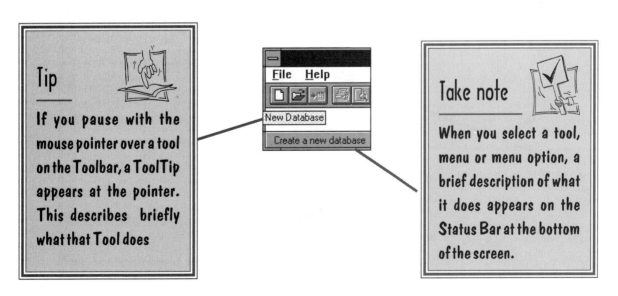

Tip

If you pause with the mouse pointer over a tool on the Toolbar, a ToolTip appears at the pointer. This describes briefly what that Tool does

Take note

When you select a tool, menu or menu option, a brief description of what it does appears on the Status Bar at the bottom of the screen.

Help on the Dialog Boxes

If you find yourself in a dialog box, and you need help on how to complete it, context sensitive Help is always available.

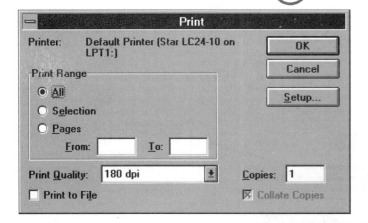

1 Press F1

1 From the dialog box, press **[F1]**. You are taken directly to its Help Page

2 Move through the on-line help until you find what you need

3 When you're finished with the Help, double click its control menu button to close it

❑ You are returned to the dialog box

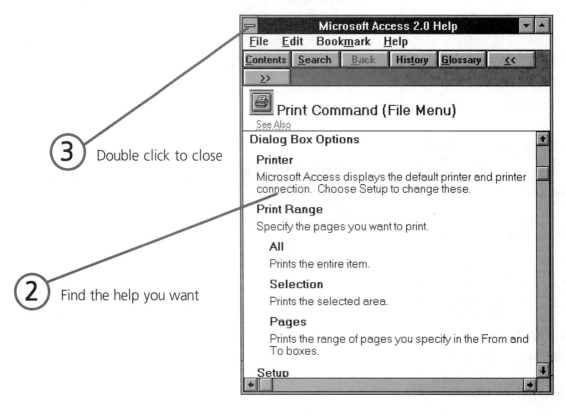

3 Double click to close

2 Find the help you want

Basic steps

Cue Cards

1 Click the **Cue Card** icon to display the Cue Cards

2 Select the topic you want help with from the list provided

3 When you reach the Cue Card that tells you what you need to know, you can continue to work on your database as you view the cards.

4 When you decide you no longer need to view the cards, double click the control menu box on the Cue Card title bar to close them.

If you are working on something you haven't done before, you might want to view the Cue Cards as you work.

Cue Cards can be displayed at the same time as your database, so you can keep the help you need on screen as you work.

(2) Select a topic

(3) Leave Cue Cards open while you work

(4) Double click to close

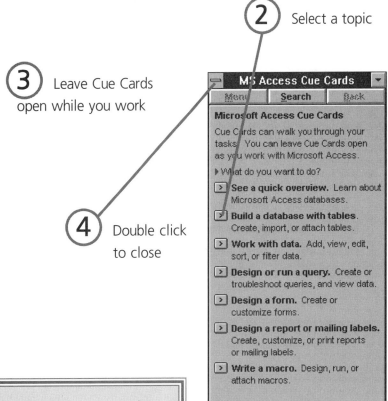

Take note

You can move the Cue Card window to a position on the screen most suitable to allow work to continue (it doesn't need to obscure your work). Click and drag the Cue Card window title bar to reposition the window.

Summary

❑ To **browse** through the Help pages, choose Contents from the Help menu, then select any topic that interests you from the list

❑ If you know what you are looking for, choose **search** from the Help menu, then use the Search dialog box to locate the help pages required

❑ To get **context sensitive** help on a **Tool**, click the help tool, then the Tool you want help on

❑ To get context sensitive help on a **menu** item, click the help tool, then the Menu, then the item you want help on from the Menu list.

❑ To get context sensitive help on a **dialog box**, press [F1] when the box is open

❑ Pause over any tool on a toolbar to display the **Tooltip** that describes the tool's function in one or two words. A brief description of the tool is also displayed on the **Status Bar**

❑ To display the **Cue Cards**, click the Cue Card icon on the toolbar

3 Building a database

Creating a new database

The first thing we have to do is create a database for our data, and give the database a suitable name.

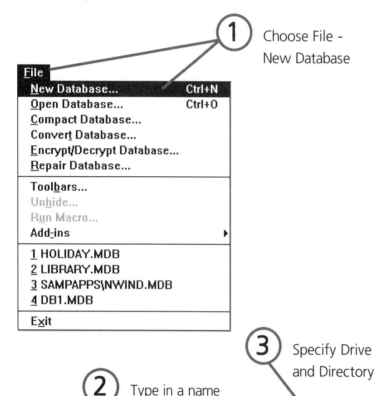

① Choose File - New Database

② Type in a name

③ Specify Drive and Directory

This should say Databases (*.mdb). Your new database will be given this extension auto- matically.

1 Click the **New Data- base** Icon ▢

   Or

   Open the **File** menu and choose **New Database**

2 At the **New Database** dialog box type a name in the **File Name** field

   The Default name is *db1.mdb* . Replace this with one that means something - in my case *Holiday*

3 Specify the **drive** and **directory** to store your new database in

4 Click **OK**

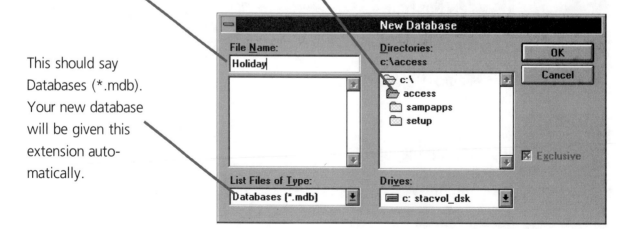

22

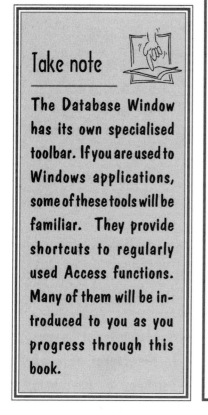
The Project

In the next few sections, I've described a project that you could work through if you wish. Though it is somewhat limited, it will demonstrate many of the Access features you need to get to grips with.

You have set up a travel service that has an extensive database of quality accommodation.

Your clients will contact you with details of:-

- where they want to go
- when they want to go
- how many people need to be accommodated
- what kind of board eg self catering, is required

You can then interrogate your database to get a list of properties that match their requirements and check prices. If a client decides to make a booking, you can get the name, address and phone number of the property's owner s, and contact them to arrange the let.

Your **HOLIDAY** Database will consist of 3 tables:

- one with **Accommodation** details
- one with **Price** details
- one with details of the property owner or **Contact**

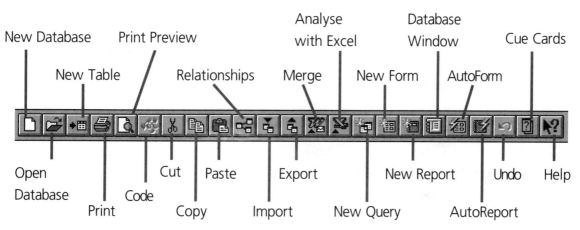

Creating a new table

The data you store will be held in a table (or tables). The table consists of

● the record **structure**, that is the Field Names, Data Types and Descriptions

and

● the record **detail**, for example accommodation details, price details, personnel details

Give careful consideration to your table structure. It can be edited (you can add fields, delete fields and change the field properties) at a later stage, but things are a lot easier if you get it right to begin with.

You must decide:-

● what **fields** you require in your Table

● what kind of data will go in the field, e.g. text, date, number etc

● which field will be your **key field** - a field that uniquely identifies the record

Once you've worked out the structure, you can then create your table.

1 Ensure the **Table Object Tab** is selected in your Database window

2 Choose **New**

3 At the **New Table** dialog box, choose **New Table**

Tip

Good planning at the start is the secret of good databases. Be clear about what you want to store and

what you intend to do with the data once it's stored.

Take note

You can also create a new table by clicking the New Table icon on the Database window Toolbar.

① Select the Table tab

② Choose New

③ Click New Table

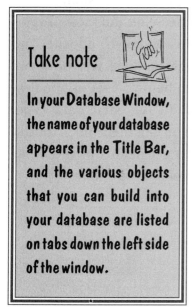

Take note

In your Database Window, the name of your database appears in the Title Bar, and the various objects that you can build into your database are listed on tabs down the left side of the window.

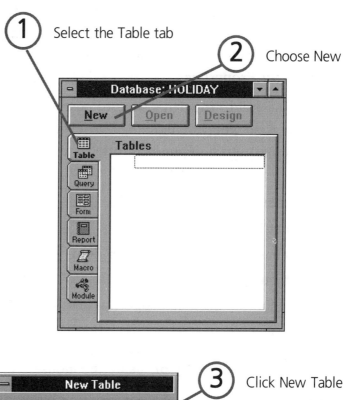

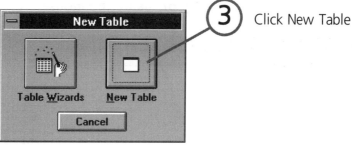

We will eventually set up three tables - the first one will hold details of the holiday accommodation we have on offer. There are different types - cottages (C), flats (F), apartments (A) and rooms (R) throughout Europe. Board is either self catering (SC), bed and breakfast (BB) or half board (HB). Properties may have a swimming pool, maid service or garden. Prices depend on the time of year.

Table design window

You will notice that the Table Design window has two panes - one that lets you specify the **Field Name**, **Data Type** and **Description**, and the other where you can specify the **Field Properties**.

You can use the **Field Properties** pane to customise the format of the field you are defining. The amount of customisation permitted depends on the Data Type selected for the field, for example

● the number of characters in a Text field

● the format in a Date/Time field

● the decimal accuracy of a Number field

● whether Duplicate entries are permitted in a field

We'll consider some of the field properties in the next few pages.

Switch between the panes by pressing **[F6]**, or using the mouse.

The table we are about to design is our Accommodation table. A summary of the fields and their properties is shown opposite. Full instructions will be given to help you set up the first field for each data type. You can then check the list to get details of the other fields of the same type.

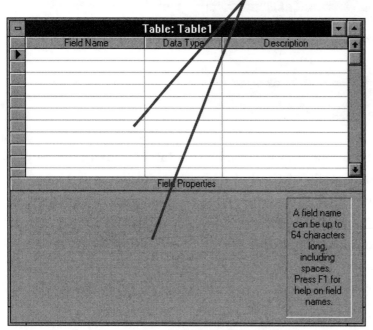

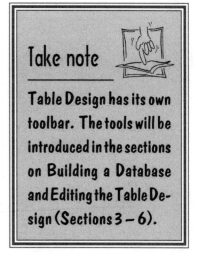

Take note

Table Design has its own toolbar. The tools will be introduced in the sections on Building a Database and Editing the Table Design (Sections 3 – 6).

26

Accommodation Table

FIELD NAME	DATA TYPE	FORMAT/FIELD SIZE	OTHER FIELD PROPERTIES
Reference	Counter	General	Primary Key. Indexed (No Duplicates)
Season Start	Date/Time	Short Date	Input Mask __/__/__
Season End	Date/Time	Short Date	Input Mask __/__/__
Country	Text	20	Indexed
Type of Accommodation	Text	1	Validation Rule ="C" or ="F" or ="A" or ="R"
Board	Text	2	Validation Rule ="SC" or ="BB" or ="HB"
Swimming Pool	Yes/No	Yes/No	
Maid Service	Yes/No	Yes/No	Default Value = Yes
Garden	Yes/No	Yes/No	
Price Range	Text	1	Description: Enter Code A-E Valid Rule ="A" or ="B" or ="C" or ="D" or ="E"
Sleeps	Number	Integer	Default Value = 4
ContactID	Number	Long Integer	Required = YES
Notes	Memo		

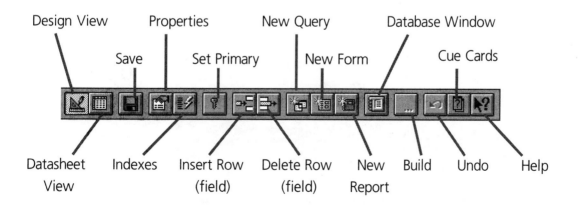

Design View   Properties   New Query   Database Window
Save   Set Primary   New Form   Cue Cards

Datasheet View   Indexes   Insert Row (field)   Delete Row (field)   New Report   Build   Undo   Help

Counter field

Our first field is the field that will contain the accommo-dation code. This code will be the unique identifier for each property - no two properties will have the same code. The field could be called something like Reference or Accommodation Code.

Fields that are used as identification fields in this way, can be completed automatically by Access by giving a **Counter** data type. When you enter data into the finished table, Access automatically puts a 1 in the *Reference* field in the first record, 2 in the second record, 3 in the third record and so on. You *cannot* enter data into the field, and Access never uses the same number twice (even if records are added and deleted later), so the field is always unique.

Basic steps

1 Type in the first **Field Name** in your Table - Field names can be up to 64 characters long, including spaces.

2 Press **[Tab]**, or point and click, to move to the **Data Type** column

3 Click the down arrow to display the list of **Data Types**

4 Choose the type - **Counter** in this case

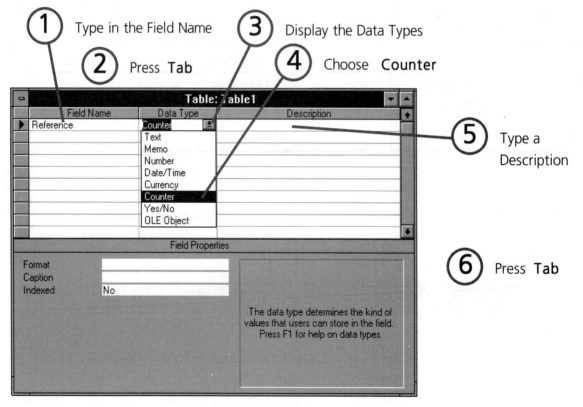

(1) Type in the Field Name

(2) Press **Tab**

(3) Display the Data Types

(4) Choose **Counter**

(5) Type a Description

(6) Press **Tab**

28

Counter Fields Property Options

5 In the **Description** column, type in the message you want displayed on the Status Bar when you enter data to this field (if you don't want a message leave it blank)

6 Press **[Tab]** to move to the **Field Name** for your next field

With a Counter Data Type, you have a choice of three Field Property options you can specify.

Number Format

In the Field Properties pane, you can specify the number format you want your counter field to adopt. If you drop down the list of pre-set formats, you can select the one that best suits your requirements.

If you prefer to specify your own format, simply key the number pattern (using permitted characters) in to the Format field. Characters that can be used include:-

0 to represent a Digit or 0

to represent a Digit or nothing

. to represent the Decimal separator

" " to represent a Literal (something that actually appears in the field)

Other permitted user characters are listed in the on-line help under Format Properties.

The Format property option also appears in fields that have a Text data type.

Pre-set number formats

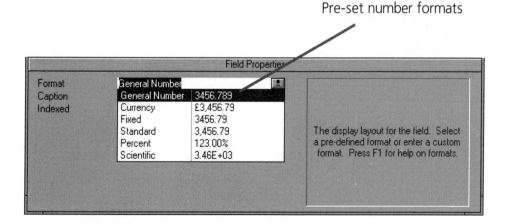

Field Properties		
Format	General Number	
Caption	General Number	3456.789
Indexed	Currency	£3,456.79
	Fixed	3456.79
	Standard	3,456.79
	Percent	123.00%
	Scientific	3.46E+03

The display layout for the field. Select a pre-defined format or enter a custom format. Press F1 for help on formats.

Caption

In the Caption field, you can type in the label you want to appear beside the field when it is inserted into a **Form**. (We will deal with Forms later in the book.) A Caption can appear more "user-friendly" on a form than a field name does. If we use a field name like *Ref*, a suitable Caption for our field might be **Accommodation Code**.

This property option is present for all data types.

Indexed

Indexing fields can have the effect of speeding up searches (although the down side can be that updates are slower). If a field is designated the **Primary Key**, this property is automatically set to *Yes, (No Duplicates)*.

This property option is present for all data types except Memo and OLE.

Take note

When specifying a Field's Properties, ensure that your insertion point is inside the correct Field in the upper pane, before you press [F6] to move to the lower pane. The current field is clearly indicated by the black arrow/triangle that appears in the selector column, to the left of the Field Name.

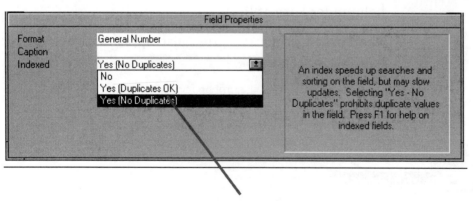

Indexed options

Basic steps

1 Type in *Season Start* in the **Field Name**

2 In the **Data Type** column select **Date/ Time** for this field

3 Press **[F6]** to switch to the **Field Properties** pane

4 Click the drop down arrow to display the list of **Format** options

5 Choose **Short Date**

6 Press **[F6]** to return to the upper pane

7 Key in a **Description** message if required (eg *"Only needed if not open all year"*)

8 Set up the *Season End* field in the same way.

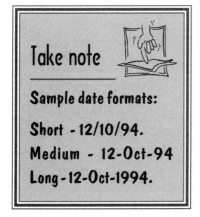

Take note

Sample date formats:

Short - 12/10/94.

Medium - 12-Oct-94

Long - 12-Oct-1994.

Date/Time fields

At our Season Start and Season End fields we are going to specify a Date/Time data type.

We will specify the format the date will take as DD/MM/YY (01/10/94 etc) - in other words we want what Access calls a Short Date format. This is specified in the Field Properties pane for the *Season Start* and *Season End* fields.

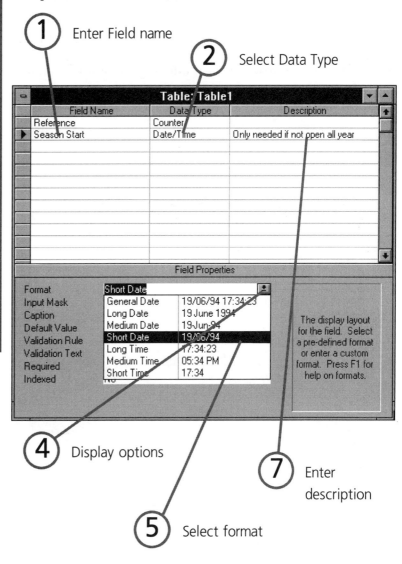

① Enter Field name

② Select Data Type

④ Display options

⑦ Enter description

⑤ Select format

Input mask

Basic steps

Regardless of how you choose to display your date, you will want to make sure that the date is keyed in accurately.

Different people might key in the same date with different separators between the day, month and year. 12/10/94, 12:10:94, 12-10-94 or 12.10.94 may all mean the 12th of October 1994 to us, but Access might not be so sure! To ensure that data entry is completed correctly, you can specify an **Input Mask**, or pattern, the data should take.

● The Input Mask does not affect the display Format.

Go back to the *Season Start* field to set up an Input Mask.

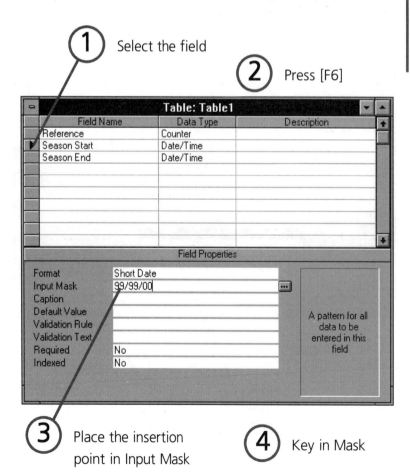

① Select the field

② Press [F6]

③ Place the insertion point in Input Mask

④ Key in Mask

1 Position the insertion point in the *Season Start* field

2 Press **[F6]** to move to the lower pane

3 Move to the **Input Mask** field

4 Key in the pattern *99/99/00* (see Table opposite)

5 Press **[F6]** to move back to the upper pane

6 Do the same for the *Season End* field.

❑ When data is entered to this field, an underscore will appear to indicate the position for each digit, and the slash character will be in place between the day, month and year sections (__/__/__) - it will not be necessary to key in the slash at data entry.

32

When setting up a pattern, you use special characters to show the type of input allowed, and whether or not input is *required*. These are listed here.

Tip

You can use a Wizard to help you build your Input Mask. If you want to try it, click the Build button (the one with 3 dots on it) to the right of the Input Mask property field. If you use the Wizard, all 3 parts of the Input Mask are specified.

Character	Description
0	Digit (0-9). Plus (+) and Minus (-) signs not allowed. Entry required.
9	Digit or space. Plus and Minus signs not allowed.
#	Digit or space. Plus and Minus signs allowed.
L	Letter (A-Z). Entry required.
?	Letter (A-Z).
A	Letter or digit. Entry required.
a	Letter or digit.
&	Any character or a space. Entry required.
C	Any character or a space.
<	Convert all following characters to lower case.
>	Convert all following characters to upper case.
!	Causes input mask to fill from right to left when characters on the left side of the input mask are optional.
\	Causes the following character to be displayed as the literal character. ie \L is displayed as L, and doesn't mean Letter (A-Z). Entry required

An Input Mask can contain up to 3 separate parts, separated by semi-colon. ie

99/99/00;0;_

The first part, *99/99/00*, specifies the Input Mask itself.

The second part specifies whether or not any literal display characters are stored with the data. *0* means that they are; *1* means that only the data is stored. The default is 0.

The third part specifies the character used to display spaces in the Input Mask. The default is the underline. If you want to use a space, enclose it in quotes ie *99/99/00;0;" "*

33

Text field

The next field in our Table is *Country*, which will hold the name of the country in which the holiday accommodation is located. This is a straightforward Text field, with a field size set to 20 (which should be long enough to store the countries we use).

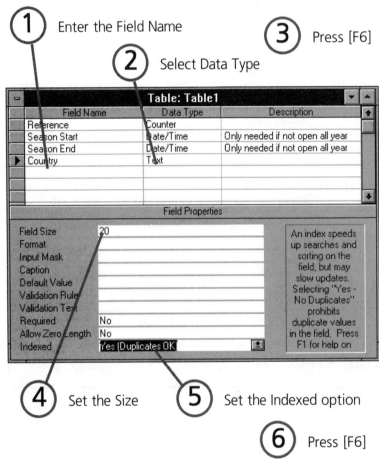

① Enter the Field Name

② Select Data Type

③ Press [F6]

④ Set the Size

⑤ Set the Indexed option

⑥ Press [F6]

Basic steps

1 Enter the **Field Name** ie *Country*

2 In the **Data Type** field, choose **Text**

3 Press **[F6]** to move to the lower pane

4 In the **Field Size**, key in the number of characters - 20 will do

5 Set the **Indexed** property option to *Yes (Duplicates OK)*

6 Press **[F6]** to return to upper pane

Tip

Indexed fields are sorted faster than non-indexed ones , though data entry and update can be slower as a result.

Country, Type of Accommodation, Board and Price Range, may be sorted, and so should all be Indexed with duplicates allowed.

Basic steps

1
Enter the **Field Name** - *Type of Accommodation*

2
Set the **Data Type** to **Text**.

3
Press **[F6]** to move down

4
Set the **Field Size**, to *1* - enough for our code

5
In the **Validation Rule**, key in *="C" or ="F" or ="A" or ="R"*

6
In the **Validation Text**, type a message to appear if the rule is not met. (Or leave blank to get a standard error message).

7
Set the **Indexed** to *Yes (Duplicates OK)*

8
Press **[F6]** to go back to the upper pane

9
Key in a **Description** if required

❑ Set up the *Board* field, Size 2, and a Validation Rule on the code - *SC* for Self Catering, *BB* for Bed & Breakfast or *HB* for Half Board.

Validation Rule property option

The *Type of Accommodation* field is also a Text field. It can be a cottage, flat, apartment or room. We'll use a one character code for each type C, F, A or R. To avoid falling into the "rubbish in rubbish out" problem, we'll set a validation rule for this field, so that only the recognised codes can be entered.

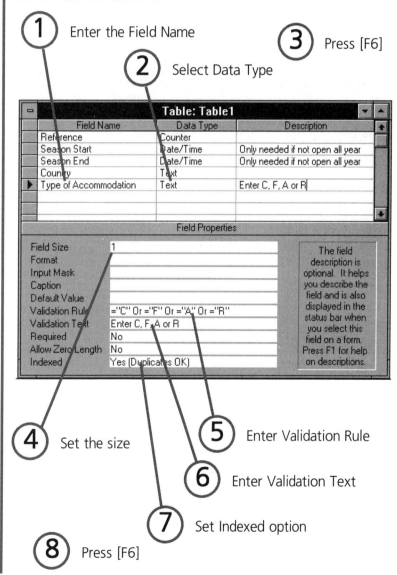

① Enter the Field Name

② Select Data Type

③ Press [F6]

④ Set the size

⑤ Enter Validation Rule

⑥ Enter Validation Text

⑦ Set Indexed option

⑧ Press [F6]

Yes/No field

If a field can have one of two values in it, eg *Yes* or *No*, *True* or *False*, *On* or *Off*, choose the **Yes/No** Data Type. The next three fields – Swimming Pool, Maid Service and Garden – are all Yes/No fields.

1 Type in the **Field Name** - *Swimming Pool*

2 Set the **Data Type** to **Yes/No**

3 Press **[F6]** to move to the lower pane

4 Drop down the list of possible **formats**

5 Choose the one required

6 Press **[F6]** to return to the upper pane

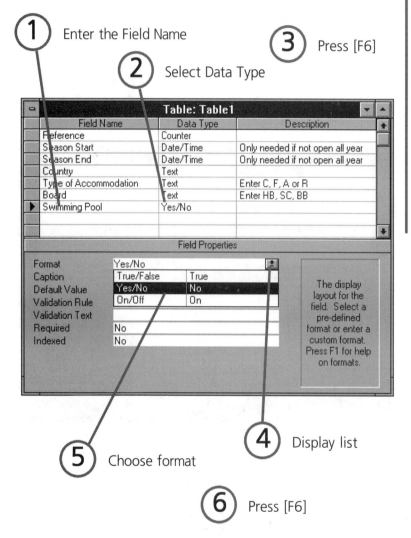

① Enter the Field Name

③ Press [F6]

② Select Data Type

④ Display list

⑤ Choose format

⑥ Press [F6]

Table: Table1

Field Name	Data Type	Description
Reference	Counter	
Season Start	Date/Time	Only needed if not open all year
Season End	Date/Time	Only needed if not open all year
Country	Text	
Type of Accommodation	Text	Enter C, F, A or R
Board	Text	Enter HB, SC, BB
Swimming Pool	Yes/No	

Field Properties

Format	Yes/No	
Caption	True/False	True
Default Value	Yes/No	No
Validation Rule	On/Off	On
Validation Text		
Required	No	
Indexed	No	

The display layout for the field. Select a pre-defined format or enter a custom format. Press F1 for help on formats.

Take Note

The default format for a Yes/No field is Yes/No. You don't actually need to do basic steps 3-6 unless you want to specify a True/False or On/Off format.

Basic steps

1 Place the insertion point in the *Maid Service* field

2 Press **[F6]** to move to the lower pane

3 In the **Default Value**, type *Yes*

4 Press **[F6]** to move back to the upper pane

❑ Set up the *Garden* field in the same way as the *Swimming Pool* field.

Default value

The default value in a Yes/No field is *No*. As we know that most of our holiday accommodation has Maid Service, we can change the default value to *Yes* by typing *Yes* in the Default Value field of the lower pane for that field.

① Go to Maid Service

② Press [F6]

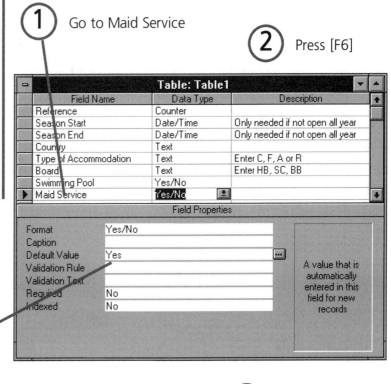

③ Key in Yes

④ Press [F6]

Take note

You will also have a 1 character Text field to set up for the Price Range field. This field could have a Validation Rule set to check that the appropriate range of codes are used - ="A" or ="B" or ="C" or ="D" or ="E"

Number field

In a Number field, you can specify the accuracy of the number that can be entered, by setting the Field Size property. In this example we have two number fields to set up - *Sleeps* and *ContactID*. With the *Sleeps* field, which holds how many people can be accommodated, the Field Size can be set to an **Integer** (you can't get 2.3 people!). With the *ContactID* field we must set the Field Size property to a **Long Integer**, as this field will eventually be used to set up a relationship between this table and the *Contacts* table.

As most of the holiday accommodation sleeps 4, we can set 4 as the Default Value for the field. On data entry, the field will be completed automatically, and it will only need editing when the number is something other than 4.

Basic steps

1 Key in the **Field Name** – *Sleeps*

2 Set the **Data Type** to **Number**

3 Press **[F6]** to move to the lower pane

4 Select **Integer** from the **Field Size** options

5 Place the insertion point in the **Default Value** and key in the value required, 4 in our case

6 Press **[F6]** to return to the upper pane

① Enter Field Name

② Set Data Type

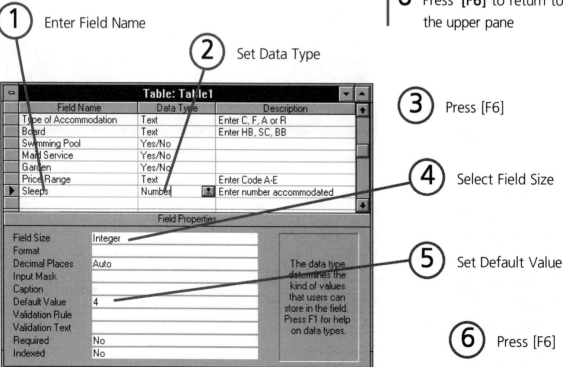

③ Press [F6]

④ Select Field Size

⑤ Set Default Value

⑥ Press [F6]

Basic steps

1 Key in the **Field Name** – *ContactID*

2 Set the **Data Type** to **Number**

3 Press **[F6]** to move to the lower pane

4 Set the **Field Size** to **Long Integer**

5 Set the **Required** property to **YES**

6 Press **[F6]** to return to the upper pane

Take note

On data entry, you will not be able to procede to the next record until you have completed the ContactID field of the record you are entering.

Required property option

As the *ContactID* field will be used to link the *Accommodation* table with the *Contacts* table, we must have an entry in it. We will therefore set the **Required field** option to **Yes**.

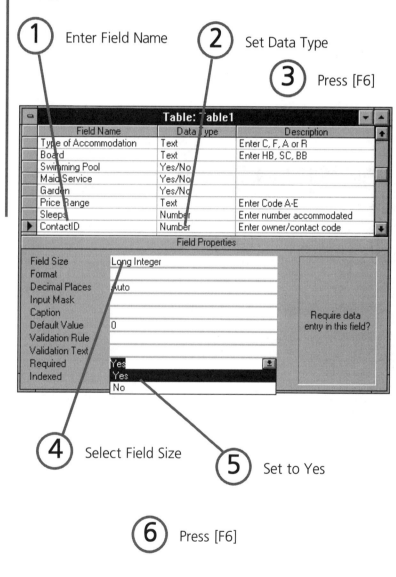

① Enter Field Name
② Set Data Type
③ Press [F6]
④ Select Field Size
⑤ Set to Yes
⑥ Press [F6]

Memo field

Memo fields are used to add descriptive detail to your records. You can add "unstructured" notes in a Memo field. You can't sort or search on this field type, but it's very useful for holding all the additional things you feel are relevant. In our example, we can add details on the location of the accommodation, the places of interest nearby, the best food and wine to sample etc (anything we think our clients might want to know!).

Basic steps

1 Key in the **Field Name**

2 Set the **Data Type** to **Memo**

3 Type in a **Description** if required

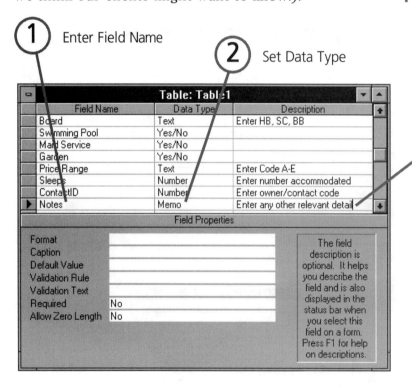

① Enter Field Name

② Set Data Type

③ Enter Description

Field Name	Data Type	Description
Board	Text	Enter HB, SC, BB
Swimming Pool	Yes/No	
Maid Service	Yes/No	
Garden	Yes/No	
Price Range	Text	Enter Code A-E
Sleeps	Number	Enter number accommodated
ContactID	Number	Enter owner/contact code
Notes	Memo	Enter any other relevant detail

Field Properties

Format
Caption
Default Value
Validation Rule
Validation Text
Required   No
Allow Zero Length   No

The field description is optional. It helps you describe the field and is also displayed in the status bar when you select this field on a form. Press F1 for help on descriptions.

Take note

Memo fields can hold up to 64,000 characters, so they are very useful for lengthy text entries when you need to add comments or explanations. Memo fields cannot be indexed.

Basic steps

1 To select a single field to become your primary key, click the row selector at the left edge of the field.

2 Click the **Set Primary Key** tool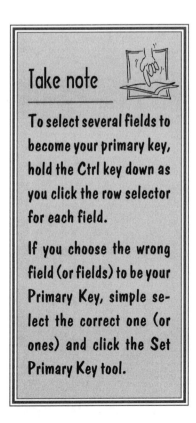

❑ Note the Key icon that appears to the left of the Key Field(s)

Take note

To select several fields to become your primary key, hold the Ctrl key down as you click the row selector for each field.

If you choose the wrong field (or fields) to be your Primary Key, simple select the correct one (or ones) and click the Set Primary Key tool.

Primary key

Once you have completed specifying your table structure, and edited any fields you want to change, you should indicate which field is to be your **Primary key.** The Primary Key is a field (or combination of fields) that uniquely identifies each record in your table.

If you don't specify the Primary Key, Access can set one up for you the first time you save your design. It will set up a field called *ID* with a Counter data type if you do this.

We will specify the Reference field as our Primary Key.

A Primary Key isn't essential, but it is strongly recommended that you set one. Primary Keys speed up data retrieval and make it easier to define relationships between tables.

① Select Reference field

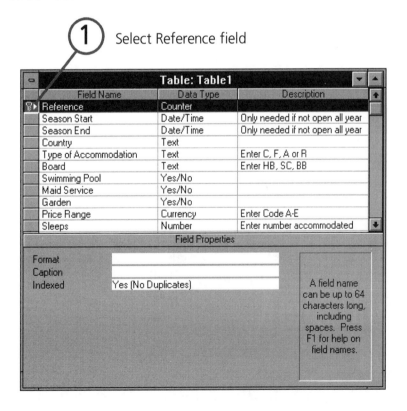

Saving the design

Once you have your table design specified, you must **save** it. Once the design has been saved, you can decide whether you want to:-

● Leave data entry till later

or

● Move into the Datasheet View, so you can enter data straight away. (See Section 5 for data entry)

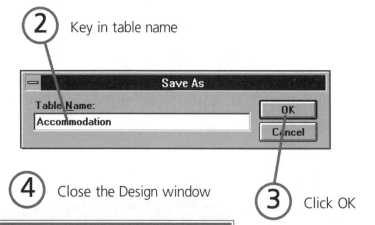

② Key in table name

④ Close the Design window

③ Click OK

Tip

Save your table design regularly as you work - don't leave it till the end. If there's a power failure, or your computer crashes and the design hasn't been saved, it will be lost and you'll have to start all over again. If you save regularly and a disaster befalls you, at least you'll have the design as it was at the last save.

❑ **Saving the Design for data entry later**

1 Click the **Save** icon

2 At the **Save As** dialog box, type in *Accommodation* as the Table Name

3 Click **OK**

4 Close the Design window by double clicking its control menu button

❑ You will be returned to the Database window, with your new table listed on the Table tab.

Take note

After it has been saved once, and given a name, you only have to click on the Save icon to save any changes onto disk.

Basic steps

□ **Saving and moving into the Datasheet view**

1 Click the **Save** icon on the Toolbar

2 If the table has not already been saved, you must complete the **Save As** dialog box.

3 Click the **Datasheet View** icon on the Toolbar.

4 You arrive in Datasheet view ready for data entry.

□ If you have gone into Datasheet view, I suggest you close the Datasheet for now and leave data entry for Section 5.

You will go back to the Database Window, with your new table listed on the Table tab.

Note your new table in the Tables list

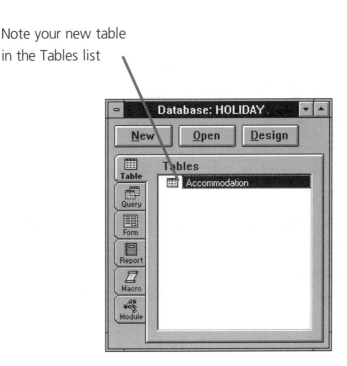

Take note

You can't exit the Design view without being reminded to save your Design if you haven't done so. If you don't want to save, choose **NO** at the *Must save changes first,* or *Save changes?* prompts, that appear.

Summary

❏ To create a **new database**, click the New Database icon on the toolbar

❏ To create a **new Table**, select the Table tab on the Database window and click New or click the New Table icon on the Toolbar

❏ Each field *must* have a **Field Name** and a **Data Type**

❏ Examples of Data Type introduced in this section are Counter, Date/Time, Text, Yes/No, Number and Memo

❏ For each Data Type, you can set various **Field Properties** as required

❏ Field Properties introduced in this section included Format, Caption, Indexed, Input Mask, Validation Rule, Validation Text, Default Value and Required

❏ Each table should have a unique field (or fields) set as the **Primary Key**

❏ You should **save your table** design regularly as you build it up (using the Save icon on the toolbar)

❏ To **close your Table** design and return to the Database Window, double click the control menu button

❏ To change from **Design** view to **Datasheet** view in your Table, click the Datasheet icon on the toolbar

44

4 Relationships

Adding a new table

We now need to set up the other tables in our database. The next one is the *Price* table. Its fields, data types and other characteristics are shown here.

Create a new table, as shown on page 24, then move to the Table Design window and define the first field.

Field Name   Price Range

Data Type   Text, **Field Size** of 1 and add the **Validation Rule** ="A" or ="B" or="C" or ="D" or ="E"

Make this field the Primary Key. (See page 41)

All the other fields have the Currency data type.

1 Key in the **Field Name** - *Jan-Feb*

2 Set the **Data Type** to **Currency**

3 [Tab] through to the next row

4 Set up the remaining fields in this way, naming them – *Mar-Apr, May-Jun, Jul-Aug, Sept-Oct, Nov-Dec*

5 **Save** the Table Design

6 Return to the Database window so we can set the **Relationship** between the Accommodation table and the Price table.

1 Enter Field Name

2 Select Currency Data Type

3 Tab to the next row

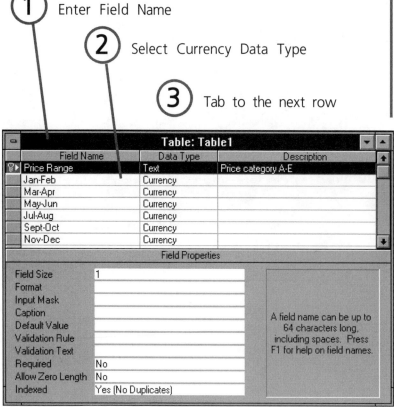

Field Name	Data Type	Description
Price Range	Text	Price category A-E
Jan-Feb	Currency	
Mar-Apr	Currency	
May-Jun	Currency	
Jul-Aug	Currency	
Sept-Oct	Currency	
Nov-Dec	Currency	

Field Properties

Field Size	1
Format	
Input Mask	
Caption	
Default Value	
Validation Rule	
Validation Text	
Required	No
Allow Zero Length	No
Indexed	Yes (No Duplicates)

A field name can be up to 64 characters long, including spaces. Press F1 for help on field names.

Basic steps

1 From the Database window, click the **Relationship** tool 🔲

or

1 Choose **Relationships..** from the **Edit** menu

❑ The Relationships dialog box opens.

2 If the Add Table panel doesn't appear, click the **Add Table** tool 🔲 to open it

3 Pick the *Accommodation* table from the list

4 Click **Add** to add it to the Relationships window. Add the *Price* table in the same way.

5 Click **Close** on the **Add Table** window

Tip

Use the tools in the Relationship toolbar to view, edit and save the relationships you set up.

Relationships

Once the table designs have been specified, it is time to indicate the relationships between the tables. Defining the relationships makes it easier to work with queries, forms and reports later on.

At this stage we want to set the relationship between the *Accommodation* and the *Price* tables. They are related through the *Price Range* field that appears in both tables.

③ Select a table   ④ Click Add

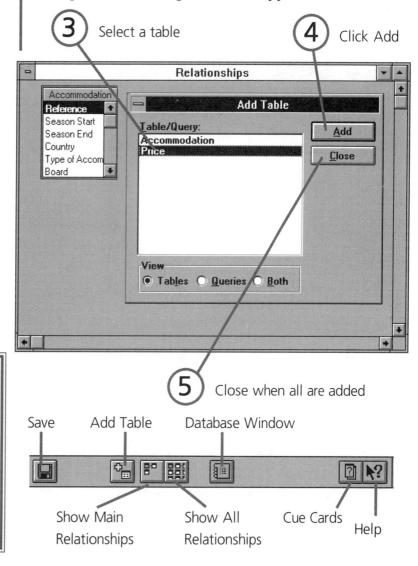

⑤ Close when all are added

Save   Add Table   Database Window

Show Main Relationships   Show All Relationships   Cue Cards   Help

Making the relationship

We must now indicate how the two tables are related. The simplest type joins a field in each table, where the same values are held in each field. A relationship will normally be between the Primary key field in one table, and a similar field in another table. In our example the Primary key of the *Price* table is related to the *Price Range* field in the *Accommodation* table.

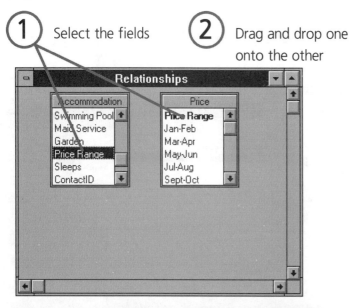

① Select the fields

② Drag and drop one onto the other

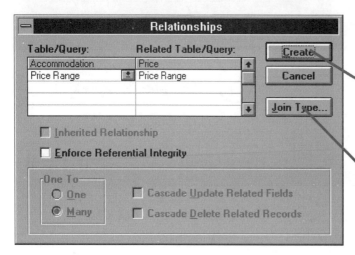

③ Click to check the type of relationship

⑥ Create the join

1 In the **Relationships** window, scroll through the list for each table until you can see the fields to be related – the *Price Range* fields

2 Drag and drop the field name from one table onto the related field in the other table

3 At the **Relationships** dialog box, if you want to edit the type of relationship, click **Join Type...**

4 At the **Join Properties** dialog box, choose the type of join required - in our case, the first

5 Click **OK** to return to the **Relationships** window, with your selection set

6 At the **Relationships** dialog box, click the **Create** button to set the relationship

❑ Now in the **Relationships** window, a line shows the related fields in your tables

7 If you want to delete the relationship, point and click on the line

8 Press the **[Delete]** key, and click **OK** to confirm at the **Delete relationship** prompt.

0 Save the relationship with the **Save** icon 🖫

10 Close the **Relationships** window

Take note

Related fields do not have to have the same name as in this example. One could have been Price Range and the other Price.

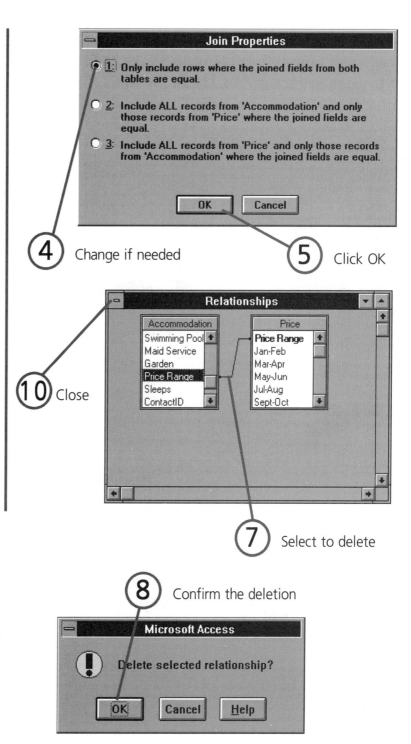

Join Properties

◉ **1:** Only include rows where the joined fields from both tables are equal.

○ **2:** Include ALL records from 'Accommodation' and only those records from 'Price' where the joined fields are equal.

○ **3:** Include ALL records from 'Price' and only those records from 'Accommodation' where the joined fields are equal.

[OK]   [Cancel]

④ Change if needed   ⑤ Click OK

Relationships

Accommodation
Swimming Pool
Maid Service
Garden
Price Range
Sleeps
ContactID

Price
Price Range
Jan-Feb
Mar-Apr
May-Jun
Jul-Aug
Sept-Oct

⑩ Close

⑦ Select to delete

⑧ Confirm the deletion

Microsoft Access

⚠ Delete selected relationship?

[OK]   [Cancel]   [Help]

49

Table Wizard

Instead of specifying your table design from scratch, you might find Table Wizard useful for some tables. We'll use it to set up our *Contacts* table for the Holiday database.

Basic steps

1 Click **New** on the **Table** tab at the Holiday database window

2 Choose **Table Wizards**

3 At the **Table Wizard** dialog box, select the type of table - in our case **Business**

4 Choose *Contacts* from the **Sample Tables** list

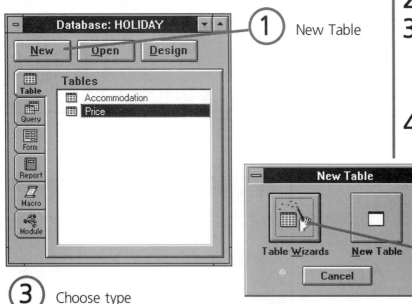

① New Table

② Click Wizards

③ Choose type

④ Select Table

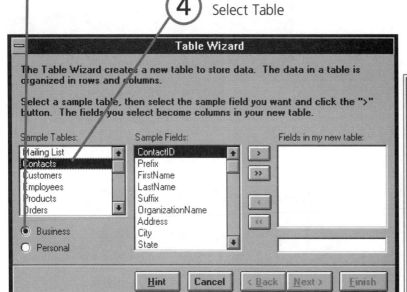

Take note

You can specify your own sample tables to add to those supplied with Access, but that is beyond the scope of this book.

Basic steps

1 Select the **Field** you want to add to your own table from the **Sample Fields** list

2 Click the **Add** field button 🔘

3 The field is added to the **Fields in my new table** list

4 Continue until you've added all the fields you need, then click

Next > to move on to the next step

Specifying the Fields

Using the table overleaf as a guide, select the fields you want to use in your *Contacts* table.

① Select field

② Click Add

③ Fields listed

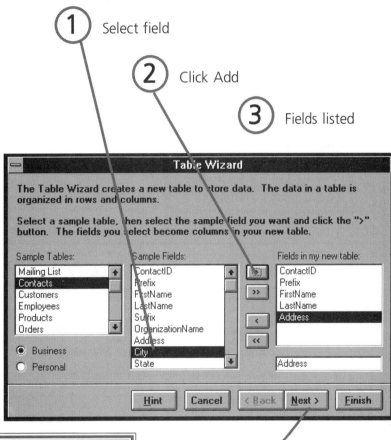

④ Go to next step

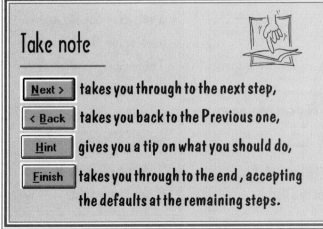

Take note

Next > takes you through to the next step,

< Back takes you back to the Previous one,

Hint gives you a tip on what you should do,

Finish takes you through to the end, accepting the defaults at the remaining steps.

Table Design

I suggest the following fields for your table. They hold the details of our property owners/contacts.

Contacts Table	
FIELD NAME	**NOTES**
ContactID	Primary Key- set this **after** fields are set up
Prefix	
First name	
Last Name	Set up using a Table Wizard therefore field attributes picked up from Wizard
Address	
City	
State	This field name is changed to *County* during set up process, or once the design is complete
Postal Code	
Workphone	Check field properties once design complete. Things like **Input masks** will need to be edited as they follow American conventions
Homephone	

Take Note

If you add a field be mistake, select it in the **Fields in my new table** list, and click the **Remove** field button

The `>>` button adds all the sample fields to the list, the `<<` button removes all the fields from the list.

New field names

❏ When adding fields to the Fields in my new table list, the field name can be changed (e.g. State to County).

1 Add the field

2 Select it in the Fields in my new table list

3 Key in the new name in the text slot below

4 Select the next field required from the sample list.

Tip

If you're in doubt about whether or not you need a particular field in your Table design, add it anyway. It's easy to remove it later if you find you don't need it after all.

You can have up to 255 fields in any table.

Basic steps

1 Edit the table name if necessary

2 Specify whether Access is to set the primary key (the default option) or you set it yourself

❏ I suggest you leave it at the default, this way the *ContactID* field is set as the Primary key, with a Counter Data Type.

3 Click

Finishing off

Once you have specified the field names for your table, the next step is to name the table and set the Primary Key.

Table Wizard will do all this automatically if you click the **Finish** button once you have added all the fields to your database (instead of the **Next >** button). It will give the table the default table name and set the *ContactID* field as the key field (with a *Counter* data type).

If you want to customise your table a bit more, or check the defaults to ensure they are acceptable to you, you can work through the Table Wizard steps making any changes necessary.

① Enter table name

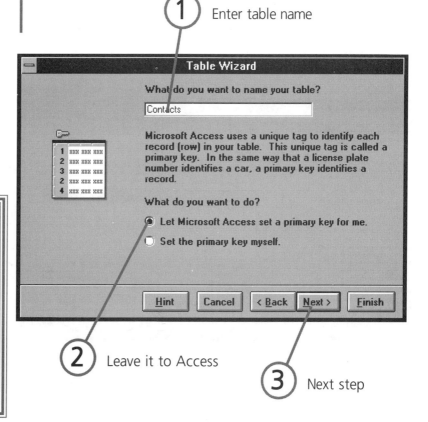

② Leave it to Access

③ Next step

Checking relationships

Normally, if a database contains more than one table, each table is related to at least one other. In our *Accommodation* table there is a *ContactID* field, which holds the code of the contact. In the *Contacts* table, there is also a *ContactID* field (set as the Primary Key) that will hold the same codes. The two are therefore "related" through this common field. Table Wizard makes this connection automatically.

The *Contacts* table is not related to the *Price* table.

Table Wizard displays a list of the tables in your database, and indicates whether or not they are related.

If you want to see how the Accommodation and Contacts tables are related, or change a relationship between your new table and one on the list, you can easily do so.

Basic steps

1 Select the table you want to check or change the relationship to

2 Click the **Change...** button

3 The current type of relationship is shown in the **Relationships** dialog box. If necessary, select an alternative option from the list

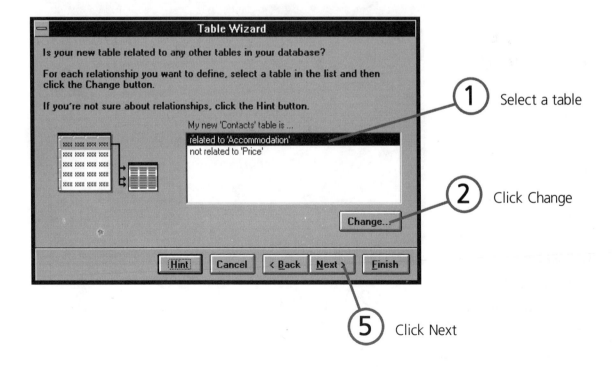

Select a table

Click Change

Click Next

54

❑ In our case, the se-
lected option, the 2nd
one in the list, is
correct. One owner
may have several
properties in our
Accommodation table.

4 Click Cancel if you
want to exit without
changing the settings.
Click OK if you've
changed a setting.

5 Once you are satisfied
that the relationships
are okay, click the
Next > button.

③ Select the relationship type

④ Click OK

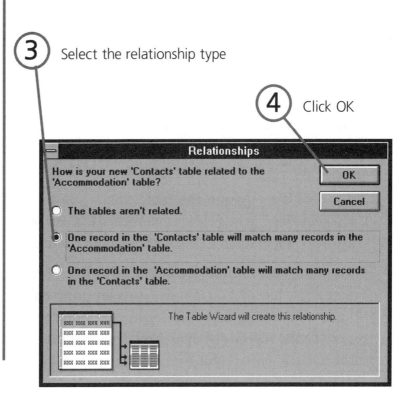

Relationships

How is your new 'Contacts' table related to the
'Accommodation' table?

OK

Cancel

○ The tables aren't related.

● One record in the 'Contacts' table will match many records in the
'Accommodation' table.

○ One record in the 'Accommodation' table will match many records
in the 'Contacts' table.

The Table Wizard will create this relationship.

Leaving Table Wizard

The last step is to choose where to go next.

● **Modify the Table Design** takes you to the Design screen, where you can change the structure of your table. We need to do this. *Postal Code*, *WorkPhone* and *HomePhone* fields all have input masks that follow an American format. These should deleted, so we can input data in our format. *State* could be changed to *County* at this stage too.

● **Enter data directly into the table** takes you to the Datasheet view. In this view, each record is a row, and each field is a column. This is the default option.

● **Enter data into the table using a form the Wizard creates for me**. If you choose this option, Table Wizard will design a simple form, that shows one record on the screen at a time. You can use either the form or datasheet to input, edit and view your records.

Basic steps

1 Select Modify the Table Design

2 Click **Finish**

3 At the **Table Design** window select a field to be modified

4 Press **[F6]** to move to the lower pane

5 Delete the entry in the **Input Mask** slot

6 Repeat for all fields as needed, then close the Table Design window

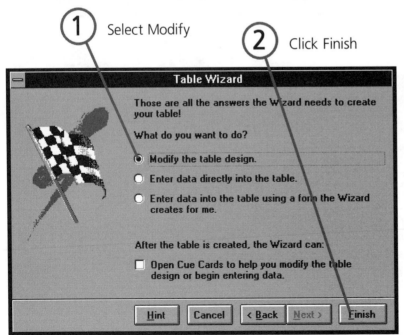

① Select Modify

② Click Finish

Take note

If you want to display Cue Cards when entering your data select the Cue Card checkbox before you click Finish. The decision isn't binding. You can display or close down Cue Cards at any time.

Closing a database

1 Double click the control menu button on the Database window

❑ Your database is closed, but you are still in Access.

If you've finished working on your database, you might want to close it. You can close a database without leaving Access. If you exit Access, any open databases are closed as part of the exit routine.

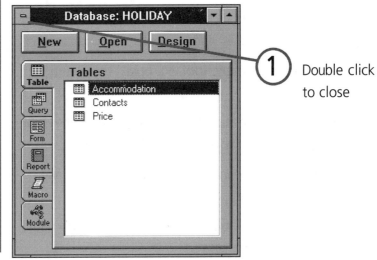

① Double click to close

③ Select a field

④ Press [F6]

⑤ Delete the Input Mask

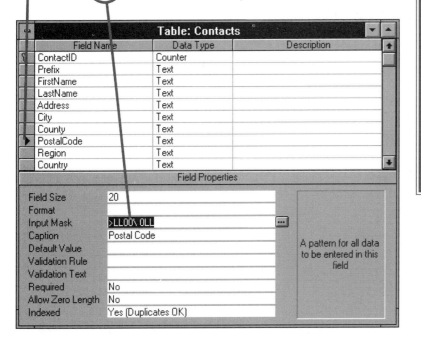

Field Name	Data Type	Description
ContactID	Counter	
Prefix	Text	
FirstName	Text	
LastName	Text	
Address	Text	
City	Text	
County	Text	
▶ PostalCode	Text	
Region	Text	
Country	Text	

Field Properties

Field Size	20
Format	
Input Mask	>LL00\ 0LL
Caption	Postal Code
Default Value	
Validation Rule	
Validation Text	
Required	No
Allow Zero Length	No
Indexed	Yes (Duplicates OK)

A pattern for all data to be entered in this field

Take note

To exit Access, double click the control menu button on the application window title bar.

Summary

- ❑ The **Currency** data type should be used for fields holding monetary values

- ❑ Most tables within your database will be **related** to at least one other table

- ❑ A relationship normally exists between the **primary key** field in one table and a similar field in another

- ❑ Click the **Relationships tool** to open the Relationships window

- ❑ To **make a relationship**, drag a field from one table, and drop it onto the related field in another

- ❑ To **delete a relationship**, select the join line and press the Delete key on your keyboard

- ❑ There are several **Table Wizards** to help automate the table design process

- ❑ To **close a database**, but remain in Access, double click the control menu button on the Database window

5 Data entry and edit

Opening a database

If the database you want to work on exists, but is not open, you must open it before you can work on it.

If you closed your database at the end of the last section, open it now so you can explore data entry in this section.

1 Click the **Open Database** tool
or
Choose **Open Database** on the **File** menu

2 At the **Open Database** dialog box, select the database to open

3 Click **OK**

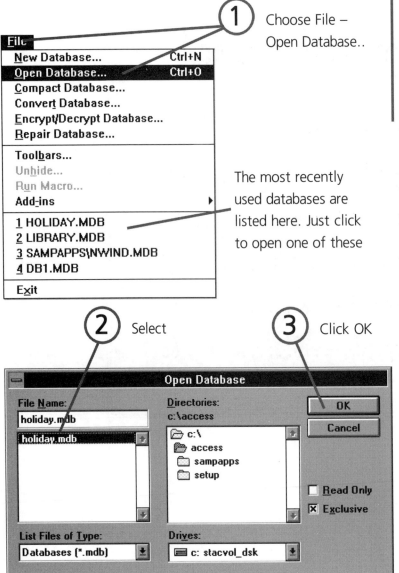

① Choose File – Open Database..

File
New Database...	Ctrl+N
Open Database...	Ctrl+O
Compact Database...	
Conve**r**t Database...	
Encrypt/Decrypt Database...	
Repair Database...	
Tool**b**ars...	
Un**h**ide...	
R**u**n Macro...	
Add-**i**ns	▶
1 HOLIDAY.MDB	
2 LIBRARY.MDB	
3 SAMPAPPS\NWIND.MDB	
4 DB1.MDB	
E**x**it	

The most recently used databases are listed here. Just click to open one of these

② Select

③ Click OK

Open Database

File **N**ame:
holiday.mdb

holiday.mdb

Directories:
c:\access

🗁 c:\
📂 access
📁 sampapps
📁 setup

OK
Cancel

☐ **R**ead Only
☒ **E**xclusive

List Files of **T**ype:
Databases (*.mdb)

Dri**v**es:
💾 c: stacvol_dsk

Tip

Double click on the database name in the Open Database dialog box to open it.

60

Basic steps

☐ **To open a table in Datasheet view**

1 Select the **Table** tab in the **Database** window if necessary

2 Highlight the table you want to open

3 Double click on the name or click the

   [**Open**] button

Take note

If you have been working in Design view on a table, you can go directly to Datasheet view by clicking the Datasheet icon on the toolbar.

Opening a table

Once you have set up the structure of your table, the next stage is data entry. The table must be open for this, and it should be displayed in **Datasheet** view (rather than Design view). In this view, each column of the table is a field and each row is a record. We will start by looking at the *Accommodation* table.

① Check the Table tab is selected

② Select a table

③ Click Open

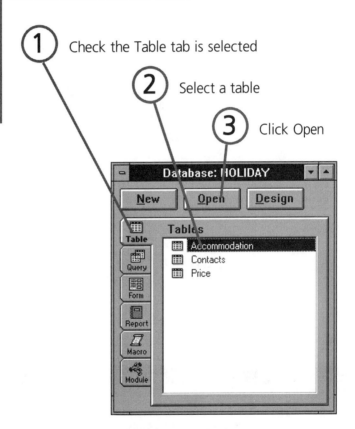

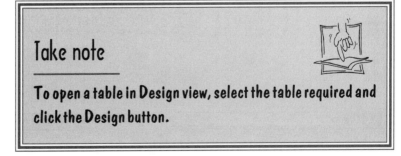

Take note

To open a table in Design view, select the table required and click the Design button.

Using Datasheet view

Move from field to field in your table using:

[Tab]   to take you forward to the next field

[Shift]-[Tab]   to take your back to the previous field

Each record is saved when you move onto the next.

Tip

If you are using the project example, there is sample data for all three tables in Appendix A.

Incremented automatically

Input Mask

Default Yes

Default No

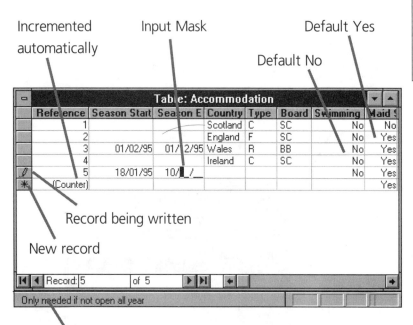

Record being written

New record

Status bar message from Description

Default No

Default 4

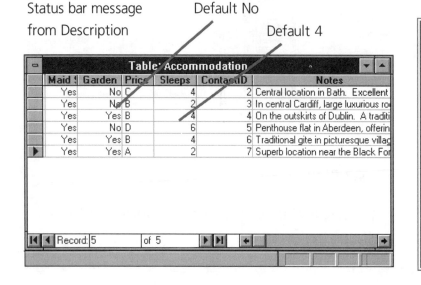

Take note

When entering data, should you find an error has been made at the Design stage, you can go into Design view to edit it by clicking the Design tool.

Editing

❑ You can edit data at any time. If you move onto a field using [Tab] or [Shift]-[Tab], the data in that field is selected.

You can then:

Replace the current contents, by just typing new data while the old is highlighted

Edit the data, by pressing [F2] to position the insertion point in the field, and using the [Arrow] keys to get to the right place.

Erase the contents, by pressing [Delete].

Inappropriate entries

If you enter incompatible data for the Data Type specified in a field (ie if you put text in a number field, or try to key something in that disagrees with the Input Mask for that field), Access will display an error message.

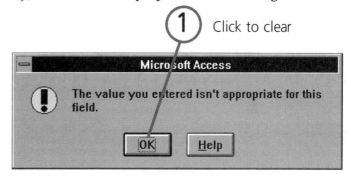

Click to clear

Moving around your datasheet

In addition to [Tab] and [Shift]–[Tab] to move between fields, there are other ways to move around.

● Point and click with the mouse to go to any field (using the vertical and/or horizontal scroll bars as necessary to bring the field into view).

● Use the arrows to the left of the horizontal scroll bar.

● To go to a specific record, press [F5], key in the record number and press [Enter].

And see the Keyboard Shortcuts, overleaf.

Go to first record

Previous record

Go to last record

Next record

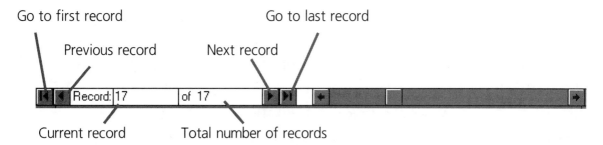

Current record

Total number of records

Adding/deleting records

Adding new records

When adding new records to your table, you add them to the **end** of the list of existing records. If you do not really want them at the end of the list, you will soon find out that it is very easy to sort the records into the order you want (rather than leaving them in input order)

1 Click the **New Record** tool ▶*

2 You are moved to the first field of the first empty row under the existing records

3 Key in the new record(s)

4 Close the datasheet or continue editing as required

(2) A new row is created at the end

Table: Accommodation

Reference	Season Start	Season End	Type	Town	Country	Board
1			C	Carrbridge	Scotland	SC
2			F	Bath	England	SC
3	01/02/95	01/12/95	R	Cardiff	Wales	BB
4			C	Dublin	Ireland	SC
5	18/01/95	10/12/95	F	Aberdeen	Scotland	SC
6			C	Lyon	France	SC
7			R		Germany	HB
8			C		Germany	SC
9			C	Brest	France	SC
10			A	Anstruther	Scotland	HB
11			F	York	England	SC
12			A	Carmarthen	Wales	BB
13			F	Edinburgh	Scotland	SC
14			C	Venice	Italy	SC
15			A		Spain	SC
16			C	York	England	SC
17			R	Nantes	France	BB
(Counter)						

Record: 18   of 18

(3) Key in records

Keyboard shortcuts

[PageUp]	Moves you up a page	[Up arrow]	Current field, previous record
[PageDown]	Moves you down a page	[Down arrow]	Current field, next record
[Ctrl]-[PageUp]	Moves you left a page	[Ctrl]-[Up arrow]	Current field, first record
[Ctrl]-[PageDown]	Moves you right a page	[Ctrl]-[Down arrow]	Current field, last record
[Home]	First field, current record	[Ctrl]-[Home]	First field, first record
[End]	Last field, current record	[Ctrl]-[End]	Last field, last record

Basic steps

1 Click in the row selector area to select the record you no longer require

2 Press the **[Delete]** key

3 At the **Delete record** prompt, choose **OK** if you are sure. The record is then deleted.

Take note

To select several adjacent records, click and drag in the row selector area until you have highlighted all the records you want to delete.

Deleting records

When some of your records become redundant, you will want to delete them. Be careful when deleting records - make sure you are really finished with them first!

(1) Select record

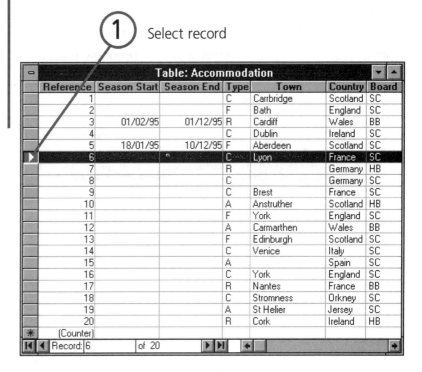

	Reference	Season Start	Season End	Type	Town	Country	Board
	1			C	Carrbridge	Scotland	SC
	2			F	Bath	England	SC
	3	01/02/95	01/12/95	R	Cardiff	Wales	BB
	4			C	Dublin	Ireland	SC
	5	18/01/95	10/12/95	F	Aberdeen	Scotland	SC
▶	6			C	Lyon	France	SC
	7			R		Germany	HB
	8			C		Germany	SC
	9			C	Brest	France	SC
	10			A	Anstruther	Scotland	HB
	11			F	York	England	SC
	12			A	Carmarthen	Wales	BB
	13			F	Edinburgh	Scotland	SC
	14			C	Venice	Italy	SC
	15			A		Spain	SC
	16			C	York	England	SC
	17			R	Nantes	France	BB
	18			C	Stromness	Orkney	SC
	19			A	St Helier	Jersey	SC
	20			R	Cork	Ireland	HB
*	(Counter)						

Table: Accommodation

Record: 6   of 20

(3) Click OK to confirm

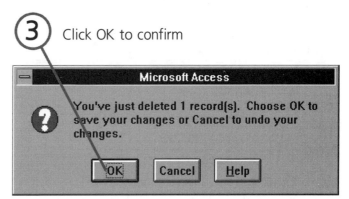

Microsoft Access

You've just deleted 1 record(s). Choose OK to save your changes or Cancel to undo your changes.

[OK]   [Cancel]   [Help]

Using Form view

If you don't like working in Datasheet view, or would prefer to see one record at a time displayed in a simple form layout rather than several records at a time in rows, try using a Form. We will look at designing forms later, but you can let Access create a simple form for you using **Autoform**. This will take the fields, and list them in a basic form, with the table name shown at the top of each record.

1 At the **Database** window select the Table for data entry

2 Click the **Autoform** tool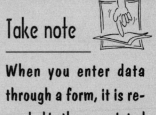

3 A simple form is displayed on the screen.

4 Use **[Tab]** and **[Shift]-[Tab]** to move between fields (or point and click with the mouse).

5 At each field key in the required data.

6 When you reach the last field, **[Tab]** takes you to the first field in the next record.

[Tab] between fields

Scroll down to other fields

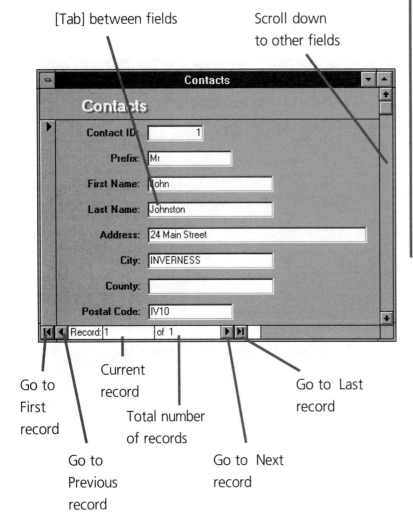

Go to First record

Current record

Go to Last record

Go to Previous record

Total number of records

Go to Next record

Take note

When you enter data through a form, it is recorded in the associated table. If you opt not to save the form, the data is still saved.

Basic steps

1
Click the **Save** icon

or

if you have closed the Form without saving, click **Yes** at the **Save changes** prompt.

2
At the **Save As** dialog box give the form a name. This can be any length and contain several word, eg *Contacts Simple Form*

3
Click **OK**

❑ The form will be listed on the **Form Tab** of the Database Window.

Naming your Form

When you have keyed in all the data, you will want to return to your Database window. Save and name the form before you go. You will be prompted to do this if you try to close without saving.

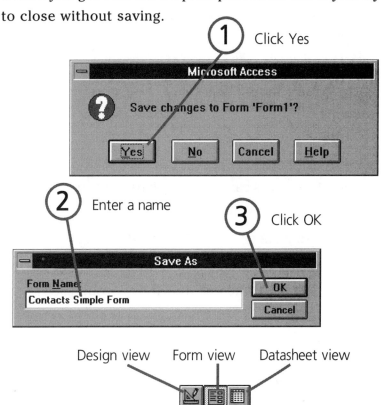

① Click Yes

② Enter a name

③ Click OK

Design view   Form view   Datasheet view

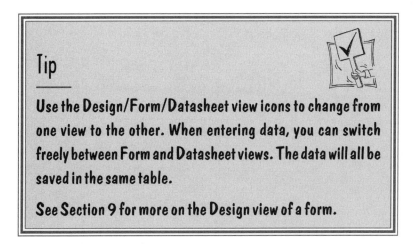

Tip

Use the Design/Form/Datasheet view icons to change from one view to the other. When entering data, you can switch freely between Form and Datasheet views. The data will all be saved in the same table.

See Section 9 for more on the Design view of a form.

Summary

❑ To **open a database**, click the **Open Database** icon on the toolbar and complete the dialog box as required

❑ To **open a table** in **Datasheet view**, select the Table tab on the Database window, then double click the table name

❑ To **move between fields** in your datasheet use [Tab] or [Shift]-[Tab], the mouse or the keyboard shortcuts

❑ To **move between records** use the arrows on the left of the status bar, or the scroll bars and the mouse, or the keyboard shortcuts

❑ To **go to a specific record** press [F5], key in the record number and press [Enter]

❑ To display your **records in a form layout**, click the **Autoform** tool on the toolbar

❑ To **change your view** use the **Design View**, **Datasheet View** and **Form View** icons

❑ The **contents of a field**, can be edited, replaced or deleted during initial data entry or at any later time

❑ To **add a record** to your table, click the New Record tool on the toolbar, then key in the detail

❑ To **delete a record**, select it, then press [Delete]

6 Redesigning a table

Adding a field

New fields can easily be added to an existing table. Try adding two fields to the *Accommodation* table.

● *Town* has the Text data type, and will fit above *Country*.

● *Star Rating* will go above *ContactID*. This field should have the Number data type and an Integer format. Add a Validation Rule set to accept only a 1 or 2 or 3 or 4 (our star rating system).

● If you are working through the project, make up some *Town* and *Star Rating* details.

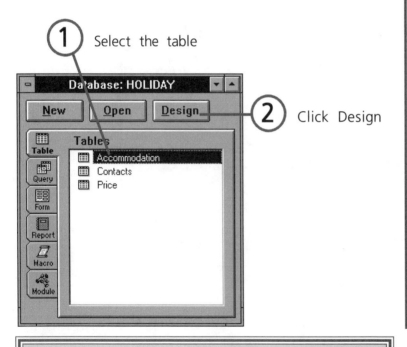

① Select the table

② Click Design

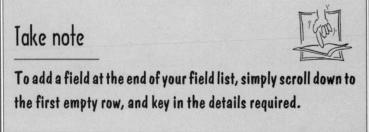

Take note

To add a field at the end of your field list, simply scroll down to the first empty row, and key in the details required.

Basic steps

1 At the **Database** window, select the table whose design you want to edit

2 Click **Design**

3 Select the row (field) that you want to have below the new one

4 Click the **Insert Row** tool

A new field is added *above* the selected one

5 Key in the detail - field name, data type, description, and set the field properties

6 Add other fields as required

7 Save the changes - click the **Save** icon 🖫

8 Close the Design window by double clicking its control menu button

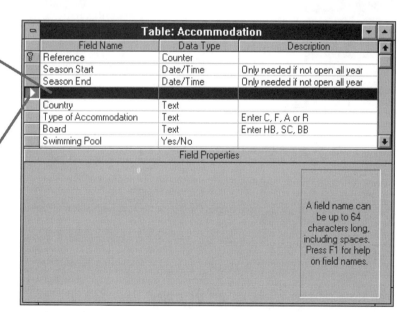

(3) Select a row

(5) Key in details

Changing the order

If the field is in the
wrong position, click in
the row selector area
and drag up or down.
Watch the thick line
that appears between
the rows to give you an
idea of where you are.
Drop it when it reaches
the right place

Deleting a field

Redundant fields are just as easily removed. Try deleting the Region field from the *Contacts* table.

Open the table Design

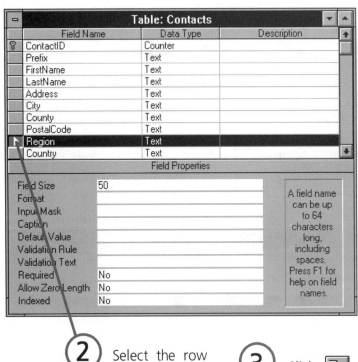

Select the row

Click

1 Open the table in Design view (see page 70)

2 Select the row (field) that you want to delete

3 Point and click on the **Delete Row** tool

❑ The row, and any data contained in that field, is deleted

4 Save the changes and close the Design window

Tip

Before deleting a field, go into Datasheet view and check the field contents. If it contains some information in any record, think carefully and be sure it is okay to delete (or you might find you have to key the detail in again!).

Changing field properties

Basic steps

1 Open the table in Design view

2 Select the first field with a **Currency** data type, and press **[F6]** to move to the lower pane

3 Drop down the **Decimal Places** list and change the property to 0

4 Do this for all the fields with the Currency data type

5 Save your changes and close the Design window

Field properties can also be modified as required. In the *Price* table, we can change the field properties of the fields with a **Currency** data type, to show 0 decimal places.

① Open the table in Design view

② Select the field

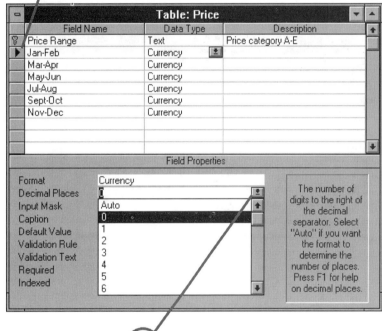

③ Drop down the list and select

Primary key and indexes

You may decide that the field that you originally set as your Primary Key, is no longer appropriate.

Changing the Primary Key is simply a case of setting a new one. (*See page 41*)

If you want to remove Primary Key status from a field, and **not** set a new one, you must use the **Indexes** dialog box.

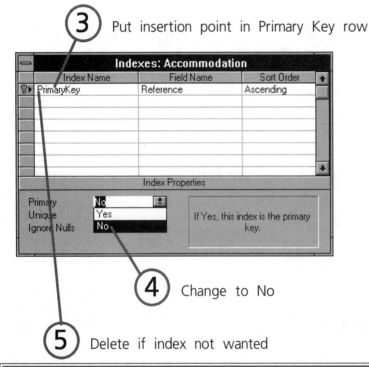

③ Put insertion point in Primary Key row

④ Change to No

⑤ Delete if index not wanted

Take note

If you remove Primary key status, the field remains Indexed, with the index name PrimaryKey. If you do not want the field indexed, either delete the row in the Indexes dialog box, or set the Indexed field property (in the Design window) to No.

1 Open a table in Design view (use any table to try this out)

2 In Design view, click the **Indexes** tool
or
Choose **Indexes** from the **View** menu

3 In the **Indexes** dialog box, position the insertion point in the **Primary Key** index entry

4 Change **Primary** to **No** - the Primary Key status is removed

5 To remove a field from the Indexes list, select the row and press **[Delete]**

6 Click the **Indexes** tool again to close the dialog box

(Set your primary key again if necessary)

Basic steps

1 Open the *Accommodation* table in Design view

2 Move the insertion point to the *Town* field

3 Press **[F6]** to go to the lower pane

4 Set the *Indexed* field to *Yes (Duplicates OK)*

5 Do the same with the *Star Rating* field

6 Save the changes

Tip

To see a list of the Indexed fields in your table, open the Indexes dialog box by pressing [icon]. You can edit the properties of any index entry - ie Index Name, Sort Order, Primary Key status etc - from this dialog box.

Adjusting indexes

Fields can be indexed at the initial design stage, or during a later edit of the design.

You should index those fields you will want to sort on or search on, as it speeds up sorting and searching.

In the *Accommodation* table, we could index the *Town* and *Star Rating* fields, as we might want to sort our accommodation on town or start rating order, or search for all accommodation in certain towns or with specific star ratings.

① Open the table in Design view

② Select the field

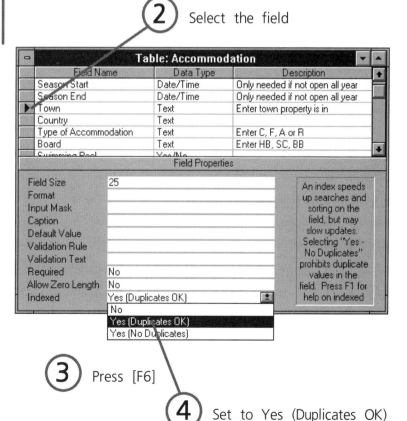

③ Press [F6]

④ Set to Yes (Duplicates OK)

Summary

- ❑ To **add a field in the middle** of your table, select the field that will be below your new field and click the **Add Row** tool on the Toolbar

- ❑ To **add a field to the end** of your field list, simply scroll down to the end of the list and key in the new field details

- ❑ To **delete a field**, select the row, then click the Delete Row tool on the toolbar

- ❑ To **reposition a field**, select it, point to the row selector area, then drag the field to its new position and drop it in place

- ❑ **Field Properties** are easily changed - position the insertion point in the field, press **[F6]** to move to the lower pane, make the changes, then press **[F6]** to return to the upper pane

- ❑ To **Remove Primary Key** status from a field, you must go into the Indexes dialog box

- ❑ Fields that are likely to be sorted or searched on should be **Indexed**

- ❑ Remember to **Save** your edited Design

7 Datasheet display

Gridlines

So far, we have been content with the way our tables appear on the screen. However, depending on the number of fields in your table, and what you want to look at, you may need to change the format of your datasheet.

You can also print data out from your table in Datasheet view, so you might want to consider customising the datasheet format before you print (covered later in this section).

By default, the gridlines are displayed between the rows and columns of your table. Most of the time this is what you want, but, particularly if you are going to print your table in Datasheet view, you might prefer to switch them off. Viewing and hiding gridlines is an on/off toggle - you switch them on and off using the same command.

It is assumed the gridlines are displayed at this stage.

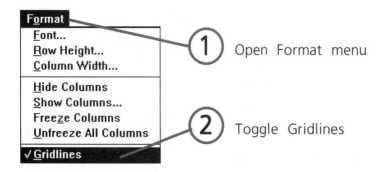

Open Format menu

Toggle Gridlines

Take note

If your gridlines are hidden, and you follow the Basic steps again, when you are returned to your datasheet the gridlines are back on.

78

Basic steps

1 Select the column(s) you want to hide

❏ To hide adjacent columns, drag in the field name row to select them

❏ To hide non-adjacent columns, do each individually or use the Show dialog box, see next page

2 Choose **Hide Columns** from the **Format** menu

Hiding columns

You may not want all the columns in your table to be visible. You may be concentrating on a task that only uses certain fields and decide to hide the ones that are of no concern at the moment, or you might want to print out only certain columns from your datasheet.

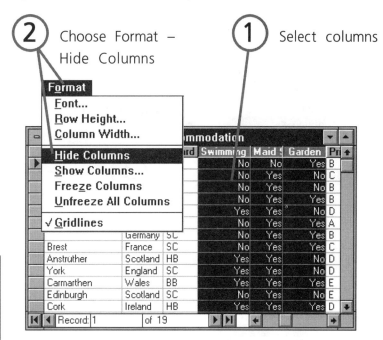

② Choose Format – Hide Columns

① Select columns

Columns hidden

Take note

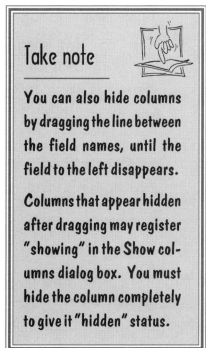

You can also hide columns by dragging the line between the field names, until the field to the left disappears.

Columns that appear hidden after dragging may register "showing" in the Show columns dialog box. You must hide the column completely to give it "hidden" status.

Showing columns

If you have hidden some columns, there will come a time when you need to show them again. The easiest way to reveal hidden columns is to use the Show Columns command in the Format menu.

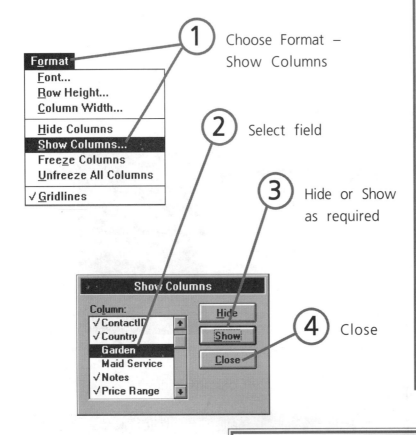

Choose Format – Show Columns

Select field

Hide or Show as required

Close

1 Open the **Format** menu and choose **Show Columns**

❑ The **Show columns** dialog box appears. The Columns currently showing have a tick beside them.

2 Scroll up and down the list to locate the field name you want

3 Toggle the show/hide status by selecting the field and clicking Show or Hide respectively

4 When you have specified which fields to show, and which to hide, click Close

Take note

You can "show" hidden columns by dragging, but it can be tricky! Locating the column border in the field name row (where one border overlays another when columns are hidden) can be a frustrating exercise using the mouse!

Basic steps

1 Choose **Font...** from the **Format** menu

2 In the **Font** dialog box, select the font, size and style

❑ The **Sample** area shows the effect your selections will have on the characters

3 Click **OK** to return to the datasheet with your new settings

Fonts

The default character style (font) is MS Sans Serif, 8 point. You may want to change this if you have been formatting your datasheet with a view to printing it. You might want to use a larger font, or make the print bold for example.

You can change the font style and/or size by using the **Font** dialog box.

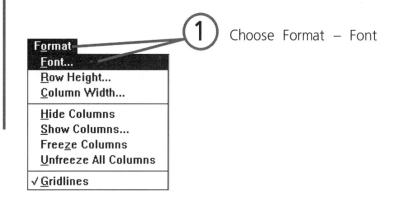

Choose Format – Font

Take note

When you change the font, it changes it for the whole datasheet, not just the column(s) or row(s) you have selected.

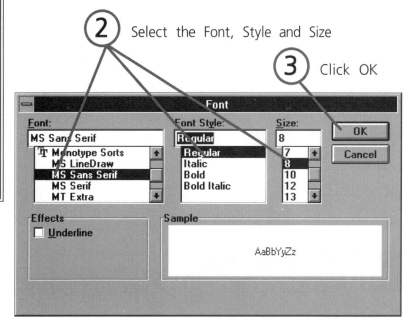

Select the Font, Style and Size

Click OK

Heights and widths

You can change the **Row Height** for all the records in your datasheet. You might need to do this if you have chosen a Font that does not fit into the current row height. Height is measured in *Points*, the same as Fonts sizes.

The **Column Widths** are initially determined by the field size or the field name size that appears at the top of each column. You can change the displayed width when in Datasheet view. Width is measured in characters.

- ❑ Setting the Row Height
- **1** Choose **Row Height...** from the **Format** menu
- **2** Set the height – or check the Standard Height box.
- **3** Click **OK**
- ❑ Setting the Column Width
- **1** Select the column(s) to change
- **2** Choose **Column Width...** from the **Format** menu
- **3** Set the required width
- **4** Click **OK**

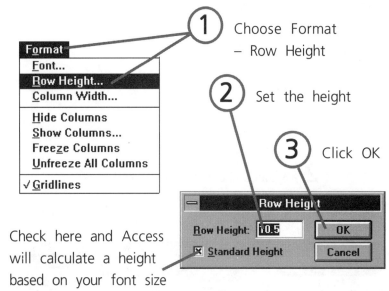

① Choose Format – Row Height

② Set the height

③ Click OK

Check here and Access will calculate a height based on your font size

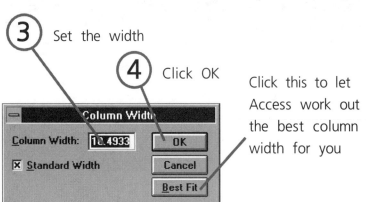

③ Set the width

④ Click OK

Click this to let Access work out the best column width for you

Take note

You can also change the height by dragging the horizontal bar between the row numbers. If you reduce it so far that you appear to lose your records, increase it through the Row Height dialog box.

Freezing columns

1 Select the column(s) you want to Freeze

2 Choose **Freeze Columns** from the **Format** menu

3 The selected column(s) are Frozen at the left of the table. If you choose columns that are not at the left, they will be moved there when you give this command.

❑ To unfreeze your columns, choose **Unfreeze All Columns** from the **Format** menu

There will be times, especially when you have many fields in your table, that you will need to view on the screen at the same time columns that are distant from each other. This can be done by hiding columns (see page 79) or by **freezing** columns at the left hand side of your screen. They will remain in position, while the other columns can be scrolled in and out of sight as necessary.

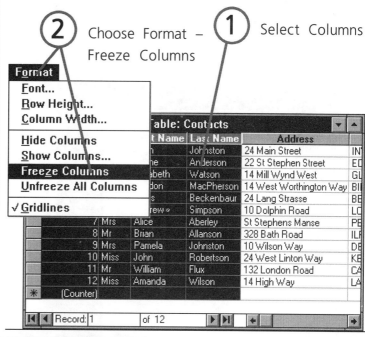

② Choose Format – Freeze Columns

① Select Columns

Thick line separates Frozen from other columns

Contact ID	Prefix	First Name	Last Name	Work Phone	Home Phone
1	Mr	John	Johnston	0463 2210	0463 1010
2	Miss	Elaine	Anderson	031 442 1021	031 556 0212
3	Mrs	Elizabeth	Watson	041 665 1043	041 510 5103
4	Mr	Gordon	MacPherson	021 557 9321	021 676 1999
5	Mr	Hans	Beckenbaur	010 49 30 121	010 49 30 435
6	Miss	Andrew	Simpson	081 475 1010	071 442 4102
7	Mrs	Alice	Aberley	091 575 3928	091 653 1843
8	Mr	Brian	Allanson	081 543 6758	071 554 1234
9	Mrs	Pamela	Johnston	0362 331112	0362 574098
10	Miss	John	Robertson	0539 561732	0539 665577
11	Mr	William	Flux	0686 203956	0686 105619
12	Miss	Amanda	Wilson	0570 30651	0570 61234
(Counter)					

Record: 12   of 12

Take note

If you Freeze columns, with no gridline display, a thick line appears to the right of the frozen columns.

Print Preview

Now that you have some data in your table(s), you will most likely want to print it out at some stage. There are various ways of doing this, but an easy way to begin with is to print from Datasheet view.

Once the datasheet display has been formatted to your satisfaction, you can print the table.

Do a Print Preview first, and check that the layout is okay on screen, before you commit it to paper.

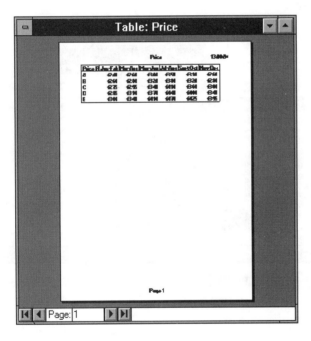

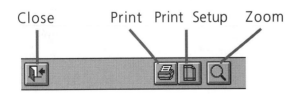

Close   Print   Print Setup   Zoom

Basic steps

1 Open the table you want to print in Datasheet view

2 Format it as required (see pages 78 to 83)

3 Click the **Print Preview** icon 🔍

❑ Your table is displayed in the Print Preview screen.

Take note

There is a special toolbar in Print Preview. You can use the tools to send your table to the printer, edit the printer setup, zoom in on your document, or close the Preview window and return to your table in Datasheet view.

Basic steps

1 Move your mouse pointer over the area of the table you want to zoom in on (notice that the mouse pointer looks like a magnifying glass)

2 Click the left mouse button

3 You are zoomed in, so you can read the data (you might need to use the scroll bars to see areas not displayed on the screen)

4 Click the left button again to zoom out

❑ The **Zoom** icon 🔍 acts as a zoom in/ zoom out toggle too.

Zoom

In Print Preview, it is very difficult (if not impossible) to read the data being displayed. This is not usually a problem, as you are really just checking the presentation of the data, not the detail. However, if you do want to check an entry, you can Zoom in to get a better look!

You cannot edit the data from the Print Preview screen - if you notice something is inaccurate or you want to change the formatting of the table, you must close Print Preview and return to the datasheet to make the changes.

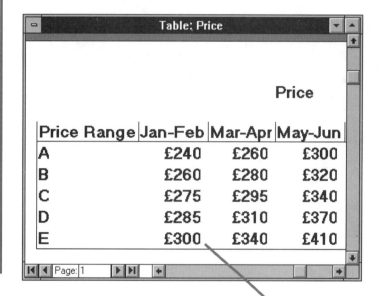

Price

Price Range	Jan-Feb	Mar-Apr	May-Jun
A	£240	£260	£300
B	£260	£280	£320
C	£275	£295	£340
D	£285	£310	£370
E	£300	£340	£410

Zooming in lets you check detail – here we can see that the numbers are being cropped and we should adjust the column width

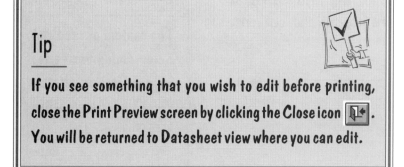

Tip

If you see something that you wish to edit before printing, close the Print Preview screen by clicking the Close icon ⬜. You will be returned to Datasheet view where you can edit.

85

Print Setup

If you need to change the margins or orientation of your page, you can use the Print Setup dialog box to make the necessary changes. You can move to the Print Setup dialog box from the Print Preview screen.

Basic steps

1 Click the **Print Setup** icon 🗋

2 Complete the **Print Setup** dialog box as required

3 Click **OK**

❏ You will be returned to Print Preview

With Landscape, you get 50% more characters on one line than Portrait

Complete as needed

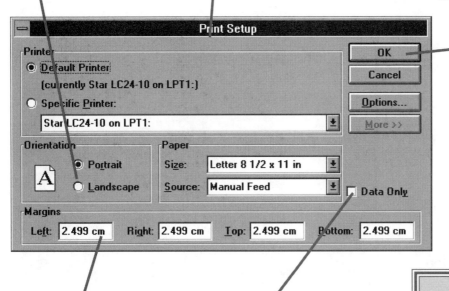

③ Click OK

Set your units of measurement to inches if you prefer

Check this if you do not want the field names at the top of the columns

Take note

The content of the Print Setup dialog box varies from printer to printer. Press F1 for the on-line help if you need it.

Basic steps

1 If you only want to print certain columns, select them first in Datasheet view

2 Click the **Print** icon

3 Complete the **Print** dialog box as required

4 Click **OK**

Printing your table

If the table is formatted and the printer setup is okay, you can go ahead and print your table. You can print directly from Datasheet view, or from the Print Preview screen. Either way, the routine is the same.

3 Complete as needed

4 Click OK

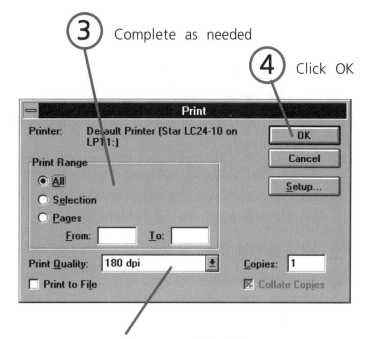

Rough draft or final quality printing?

Take note

In the Print Range options, Selection will print only the columns selected in your table when you chose the Print command. You do not need to print all the columns.

Tip

Multiple copies are printed quicker uncollated – i.e. all page 1's then all page 2's, etc, but you will have to collate them by hand later.

Summary

❑ The **Gridlines** can be toggled on and off using the Format menu

❑ To **hide columns**, select the columns then choose Format – Hide columns

❑ To **show hidden columns**, choose Format – Show Columns and complete the dialog box as required

❑ To **change the font** used in your datasheet, choose Format – Font and select from the options

❑ To **customise the row height**, choose Format – Row Height and specify the required height

❑ To **change the width of columns** choose Format – Column Width, and set the width in the dialog box, or drag the line between the field names

❑ To **stop columns scrolling** off the screen, select them and choose Format – Freeze columns

❑ To **unfreeze your columns**, choose Unfreeze all columns from the Format menu

❑ To **preview your datasheet** before printing, click the Print Preview tool on the toolbar

❑ To **check details** on the Print Preview screen, zoom in and out as required

❑ To **change the margins**, paper size or orientation of the paper, go into Print Setup

❑ To **print your datasheet**, click the Print tool on the Datasheet toolbar or on the Print Preview toolbar

8 Sorting and searching

Find

With larger databases, it is impractical to locate records by scrolling through, reading each row. Instead, you can use the **Find** command, which will locate records that contain a specified item of text. Find works most efficiently if you know what field the data is in (so you don't need to search the whole table), and the field is *Indexed*.

Basic steps

1 If you know what field the data is in, position the insertion pointer in it before you start

2 Click the **Find** icon
   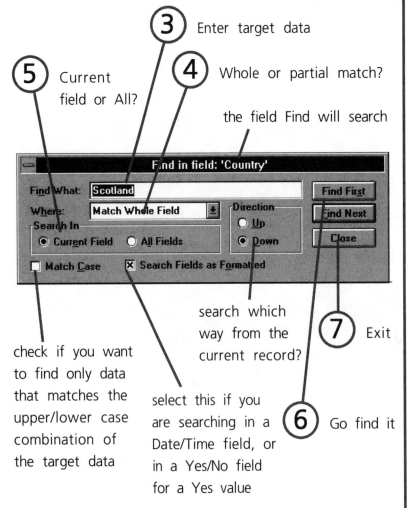 The **Find** dialog box appears. Drag on its title bar to move it so that does not obscure the data you are working with.

3 Key the target data in the **Find What:** slot

4 In **Where:** indicate where the data appears in the field

5 In **Search In** , specify whether to search in the **Current** field, or **All** fields

6 Click ⟨Find First⟩ to start the search, or
   ⟨Find Next⟩ after you have found one and want the next match

7 When you have found all you want, click
   ⟨Close⟩

③ Enter target data

⑤ Current field or All?

④ Whole or partial match?

the field Find will search

check if you want to find only data that matches the upper/lower case combination of the target data

select this if you are searching in a Date/Time field, or in a Yes/No field for a Yes value

search which way from the current record?

⑦ Exit

⑥ Go find it

90

Basic steps

1 Click the **Edit Sort/ Filter** icon

2 In the **Sort/Filter** dialog box, select your first field from the list

3 For the **Criteria** enter the data you are looking for

4 Repeat for the other fields

5 Click the **Apply Sort/ Filter** icon

❑ A subset of records that meet the criteria are displayed

Multi-field selection

When working on a table, you will sometimes want to select records based on the information held in several fields, eg you might want to view all the properties that offer self catering facilities (*SC*) in *Scotland*.

Find only works for one search item. When you have several criteria, you must use the **Sort/Filter** dialog box. At the simplest, this is just a matter of telling Access which fields to search, and what to look for in each.

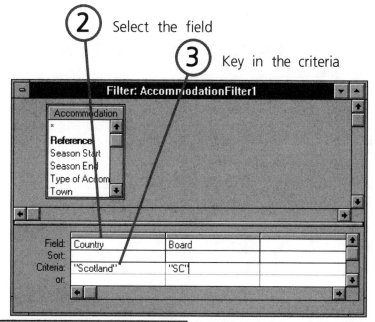

② Select the field

③ Key in the criteria

Tip

To view all your records again, click the **Show All Records** icon.

91

Editing the criteria

You can easily edit the criteria you have set if you discover you are not getting the results you expected, or if you want carry out a search using different criteria.

On the other hand, if you have set up a complex filter and it produces just the set of records you wanted, and you are likely to want the same set again in future, you can save the set of criteria as a Query. This will be stored on disk, with the rest of the database and can be run again whenever it is wanted. (See page 95, *Saving queries*.)

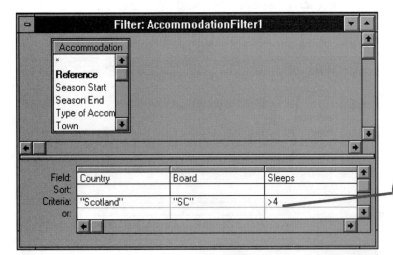

❑ **Editing criteria**

1 Click the **Edit Sort/ Filter** icon

2 Edit existing fields and criteria or add new ones as required - in this example the new criteria is that the number in the Sleeps field is greater then 4

3 Click the **Apply Sort/ Filter** icon

2 Add or edit criteria as required

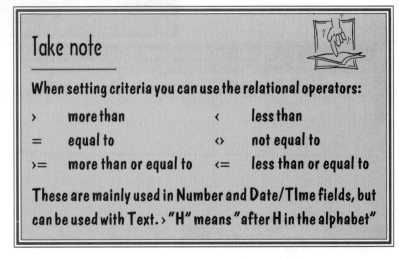

Take note

When setting criteria you can use the relational operators:

>	more than	‹	less than
=	equal to	‹›	not equal to
›=	more than or equal to	‹=	less than or equal to

These are mainly used in Number and Date/TIme fields, but can be used with Text. ›"H" means "after H in the alphabet"

Basic steps

Sort

1 Open the table you want to sort (in our case *Accommodation*)

2 Put the insertion point anywhere in the field you want to sort your records on

3 Click the Ascending Sort [A/Z] or Descending Sort [Z/A] icon

❏ The records are re-arranged as indicated

When you key records into a table, they appear in the order they were input, or that of the primary key if one is set. There will be times when you need the records in a different order, ascending or descending, using some other field in the table. For example, in the *Accommodation* table, you might decide to re-arrange, or **sort**, your records into *Country*, *Town* or *Star Rating* order.

Sorting your records on one field is very easy. We could use the *Accommodation* table to try this out.

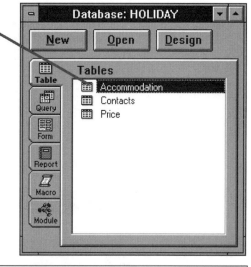

① Open in Datasheet view

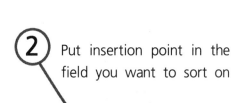

② Put insertion point in the field you want to sort on

Take note

You can be anywhere, in any row, in the field you want to sort on. The whole table will be sorted in the requested order (ascending or descending) of the data in that field.

Multi-level sorts

If you need to sort your table on more than one field, you have to set the sort up in the **Sort/Filter** dialog box.

Multi-level sorts are very useful, when for example, you have a table of clients, where you want to sort the records primarily by *Country*, then by *City*, then by *Company*. Multi-level sorts take longer than one field sorts, and obviously the more levels you sort to, the longer it takes.

We'll do a simple multi-level sort, rearranging the records in the *Accommodation* table by *Country*, then by *Town*.

1 Open the table you want to sort (in our case *Accommodation*)

2 Click the **Edit Sort/ Filter** icon

3 In the **Filter** dialog box, indicate the fields you want to sort onby double-clicking on each in the Field list

4 For each chosen field, click in the **Sort** row, drop down the sort options and select the one required

5 Click the **Apply Sort/ Filter** icon

6 The sorted table is displayed

③ Specify the fields

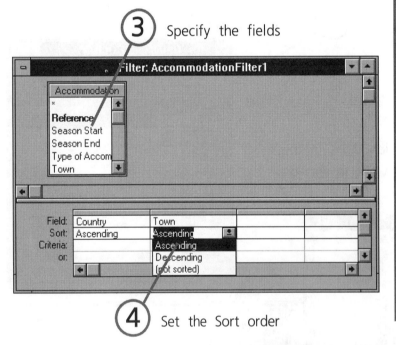

④ Set the Sort order

Records sorted by Country, then by Town

	Reference	Town	Country	Board	Swimming
▶	2	Bath	England	SC	N
	11	York	England	SC	Ye
	16	York	England	SC	N
	9	Brest	France	SC	N
	17	Nantes	France	BB	N
	8		Germany	SC	N
	7		Germany	HB	N
	20	Cork	Ireland	HB	Ye

Table: Accommodation
Record: 1 of 19

94

Basic steps

1 From the **Filter** dialog box, click the **Save** icon

2 At the **Save As Query** dialog box, enter a meaningful name for the sort – any length and having several words if you like

3 Click **OK**

❑ When you return to the **Database** window, you will find the Query located on the **Query** Tab.

If you have set up a complex sort, you might want to save it, so you can use it again. We can save the Sort/Filter definition as a Query.

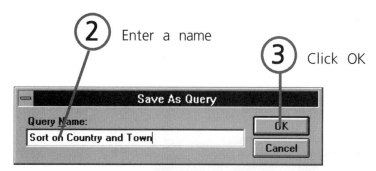

② Enter a name

③ Click OK

Save As Query

Query Name:
Sort on Country and Town

OK
Cancel

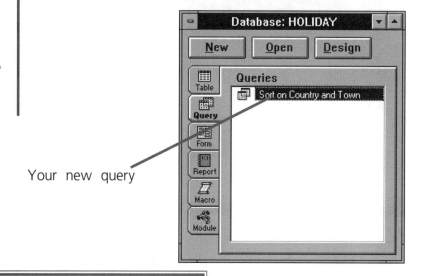

Database: HOLIDAY

New   Open   Design

Queries

Sort on Country and Town

Table
Query
Form
Report
Macro
Module

Your new query

Take note

If you have applied your Filter/Sort criteria, and then decide you want to save the criteria as a Query, you can click the Edit sort/filter tool to return to the Filter dialog box, where the criteria will still be set up. You can then save the criteria.

Reusing queries

Sometimes you will want to rerun an existing query without alteration; sometimes you may want to make a minor adjustment to a query before reusing it; other times it is quicker to start from scratch with a new one.

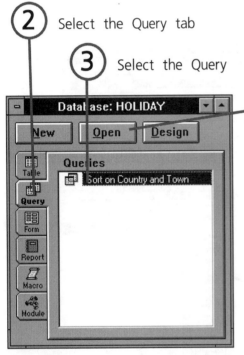

② Select the Query tab

③ Select the Query

④ Click Open

Basic steps

❑ **Running a Query**

1 Open the Database window

2 Select the **Query** tab

3 Select the Query name

4 Click   **Open**

❑ The table is opened, listing the records in the order set by the sort criteria, or the sub-set of records selected by a filter

	Table: Accommodation			
Reference	Town	Country	Board	Swimming
2	Bath	England	SC	N
11	York	England	SC	Ye
16	York	England	SC	N
9	Brest	France	SC	N
17	Nantes	France	BB	N
8		Germany	SC	N
7		Germany	HB	N
20	Cork	Ireland	HB	Ye

Record: 1   of 19

Tip

You can double click the query name on the Query tab to open the query and run it.

96

Basic steps

1 Open the Database window

2 Select the **Query** tab

3 Select the Query name

4 Click [**Design**]

5 At the **Select Query** dialog box check and update your sort or selection criteria as necessary.

6 **Save** the Query and/or Run it ▮

Editing a Query from the Database window

The process is identical to normal Query editing, except that you are working in the **Select Query** dialog box. New criteria may be added, and existing ones removed or changed.

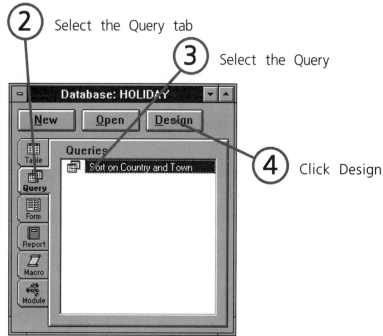

② Select the Query tab

③ Select the Query

④ Click Design

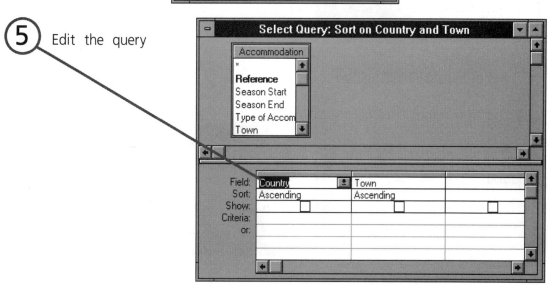

⑤ Edit the query

Multi-table queries

If you have more than one table in your database, there will come a time when you need to interrogate several tables at the same time in order to locate the information you require. To do this in Access you set up a **Query**. The Sort/Filter feature allows you to interrogate the current table, and you can *save* the Sort/Filter criteria as a Query. When working with more than one table, you *start* out by setting up a Query.

This example draws data from three tables. I want to find properties that sleep more than 4, and for each matching property, I want details of:-

● what Town the property is in (*Accommodation*)

● the Contact's name and phone number (*Contacts*)

● the cost of the property in May/June (*Price*)

You can build up a Query from the Database window.

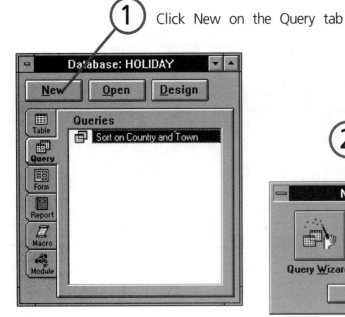

① Click New on the Query tab

② Click New Query

❑ **Adding the tables**

1 Click the **New Query** icon in the Database window

or

1 Click [**New**] on the Query tab

2 At the **New Query** dialog box, choose **New Query**. This opens the **Select Query** dialog box, where you specify the tables you want to query and set up your criteria

3 The **Add Table** dialog box should be open. If it is not, click the **Add Table** Icon

Join lines

4 Select the table(s) that you want to query, one at a time. Click [**Add**] to add them to the Select Query dialog box

5 When all the tables have been added, click [**Close**] to close the **Add Table** dialog box.

Selected tables and their join lines are shown in the upper pane

In the upper half of the Select Query dialog box, the join-lines between the tables are displayed. These lines indicate the fields that relate one table to another. We can see that the *Accommodation* and *Contacts* tables are related through the *ContactID* field. The *Accommodation* table and the *Price* table are related through the *Price Range* field. The primary key in each table is displayed in bold type in the field list.

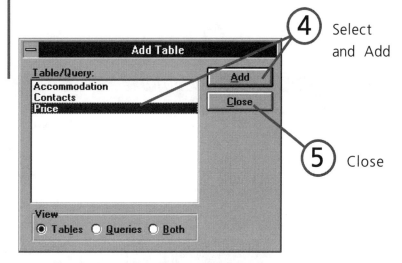

④ Select and Add

⑤ Close

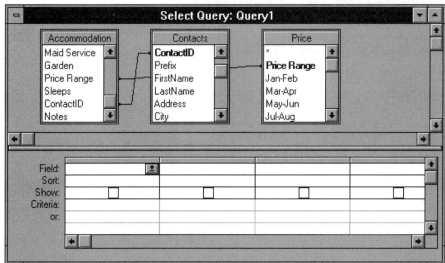

Specifying the Query criteria

The next stage is to select fields to be included in the output, and to specify any criteria that are to be used to select records. We want the *Town* and *Sleeps* fields from *Accomodation*, with the criteria *>4* (more than 4) set for *Sleeps*; *Prefix, Last Name* and *HomePhone* from *Contacts*; and *May-Jun* from *Price*. If we set **Sort** criteria, we can also determine the order of records in the final output.

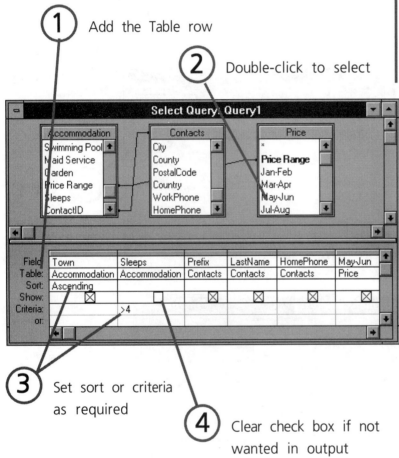

① Add the Table row

② Double-click to select

③ Set sort or criteria as required

④ Clear check box if not wanted in output

1 Click the **Table Names** icon 🔲 to add a Table row to the field information area in the lower half of the dialog box

2 Select fields for inclusion by double-clicking on them in their table lists.

3 Set the sort and/or selection criteria (if required)

4 If you do **not** want to display the field contents when you run the query, click the **Show** checkbox to remove the cross

5 Save the Query 🔲.

6 Give the Query a suitable name

7 Click **OK**

8 Apply the new Query by, clicking the Run It icon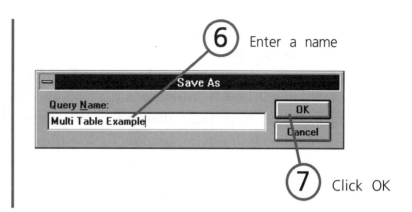

9 Close the Query

❑ The result is shown as a table in Datasheet view

Take note

The Query can be found on the Query Tab in the Database window

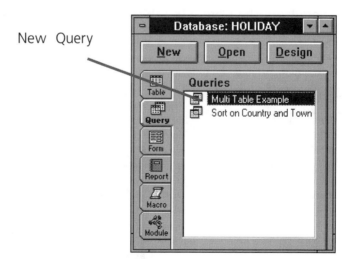

Query Wizard

When we were building up tables, we found there was a Table Wizard to help. There is also a Wizard to take you through the process of building up a query. With the Query Wizard, you'll find it provides a useful way of creating rather complex queries - queries that you might otherwise find difficult, if not impossible, to do without spending much more time learning Access.

To demonstrate the Query Wizard feature, we will build a query that will interrogate both the *Contacts* and *Accommodation* tables. We want to find out if we have any Contacts listed in our Contacts table, who no longer have entries in the Accommodation table.

This is a query we might want to run occassionally, to help us update our *Contacts* table. Once we have identified any contacts that are no longer active, we might then want to get in touch with them to establish that they have no properties available, and if this is the case, perhaps delete them from the Contacts table.

Basic steps

1 Click the **New Query** icon 🔳 in the Database window

or

1 Click [**New**] on the Query tab

2 Choose **Query Wizards** from the **New Query** dialog box

3 Choose **Find Unmatched Query** from the list of Query Wizards (look at the others at your leisure)

4 Click **OK**

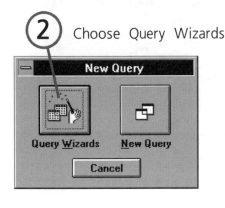

② Choose Query Wizards

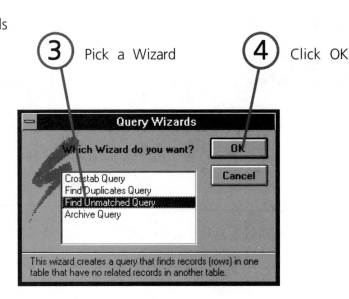

③ Pick a Wizard

④ Click OK

Basic steps

Providing the information required by the Wizard

1 Specify the table that has the detail we want in our result table (*Contacts* in our case)

2 Click [**Next >**]

3 Specify the table to look for unmatched records in (*Accommo-dation* in our case)

4 Click [**Next >**]

We must now specify:-

● the tables to compare

● the field to look for a mismatch in

● the fields to list in the result table

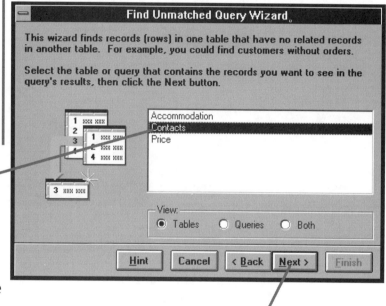

① Table to base results on

③ Table to compare

② Click Next

④ Click Next

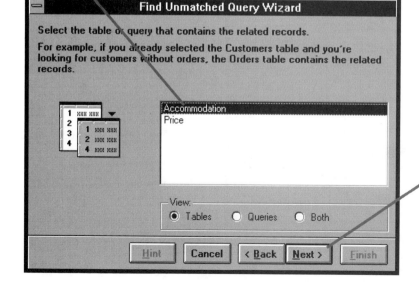

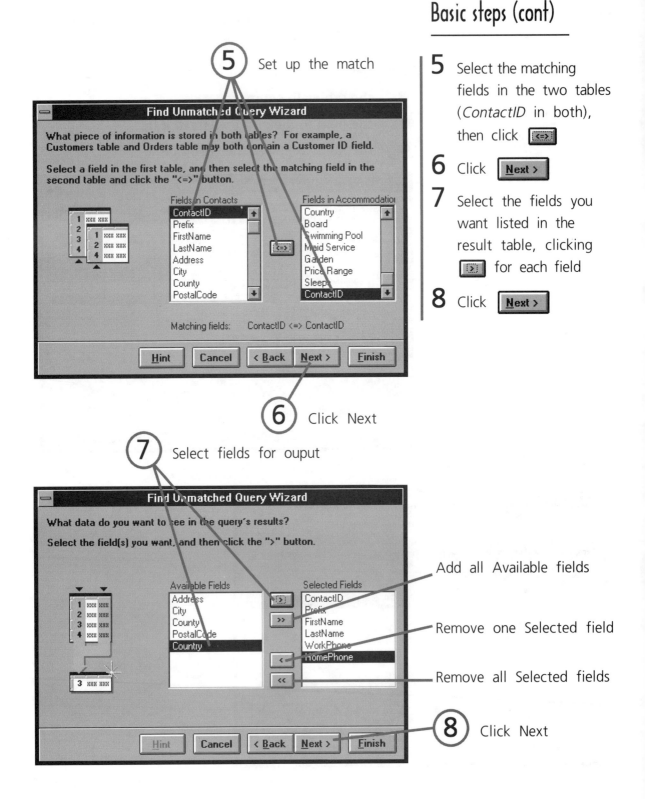

⑤ Set up the match

Find Unmatched Query Wizard

What piece of information is stored in both tables? For example, a
Customers table and Orders table may both contain a Customer ID field.

Select a field in the first table, and then select the matching field in the
second table and click the "<=>" button.

Fields in Contacts
ContactID
Prefix
FirstName
LastName
Address
City
County
PostalCode

Fields in Accommodation
Country
Board
Swimming Pool
Maid Service
Garden
Price Range
Sleeps
ContactID

Matching fields: ContactID <=> ContactID

Hint   Cancel   < Back   Next >   Finish

⑥ Click Next

⑦ Select fields for ouput

Find Unmatched Query Wizard

What data do you want to see in the query's results?

Select the field(s) you want, and then click the ">" button.

Available Fields
Address
City
County
PostalCode
Country

Selected Fields
ContactID
Prefix
FirstName
LastName
WorkPhone
HomePhone

Hint   Cancel   < Back   Next >   Finish

Add all Available fields

Remove one Selected field

Remove all Selected fields

⑧ Click Next

5 Select the matching
fields in the two tables
(*ContactID* in both),
then click [<=>]

6 Click [Next >]

7 Select the fields you
want listed in the
result table, clicking
[>] for each field

8 Click [Next >]

Basic steps

1 Name the query, either accept the suggested name or replace it with a more appropriate one

2 Choose what you want to do next, I suggest **Open the Query to view the data**

3 Click

❑ The result table lists any people it finds in *Contacts*, who have no properties in the *Accommodation* table

Take note

If you want to see how the Wizard has set this query up, select the Query tab in the Database window, select the query name and click the Design button.

Finishing off

Okay, nearly there. You should be at the chequered flag!! All that's left to do is name the query and decide what to do next.

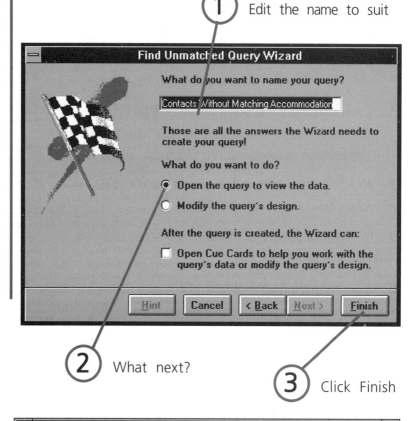

(1) Edit the name to suit

(2) What next?

(3) Click Finish

Find Unmatched Query Wizard

What do you want to name your query?

Contacts Without Matching Accommodation

Those are all the answers the Wizard needs to create your query!

What do you want to do?

◉ **Open the query to view the data.**

○ Modify the query's design.

After the query is created, the Wizard can:

☐ Open Cue Cards to help you work with the query's data or modify the query's design.

Hint | Cancel | < Back | Next > | Finish

Select Query: Contacts Without Matching Accommodation

	Contact ID	Prefix	First Name	Last Name	Work Phone	Home Phone
▶	15	Mr	Paul	Mitchell	0224 10231	0224 54123
✳	(Counter)					

Record: 1 of 1

105

Summary

- ❑ If you know what data a field contains, you can use the **Find** command to locate it

- ❑ To **sort your records** into Ascending or Descending order, place the insertion point in the field you want to sort on, then click the appropriate Sort tool

- ❑ **Multi-level sorts** must be set up in the Filter dialog box

- ❑ If you **save from the Sort/Filter** dialog box, the criteria are saved as a Query, and the Query will be listed on the Query tab in the Database window

- ❑ You can set up **criteria for a search** in the Filter dialog box

- ❑ To **interrogate several tables** at the same time, you must set up a Query

- ❑ You can use a **Query Wizard** to set up a Query

9 Forms

Designing a form

Forms allow you to customise your screen for input and editing purposes, making the screen more "user friendly".

We have already used a basic form generated by Autoform in Section 5. In this section we will design from scratch a simple tabular form, with data arranged in vertical columns; and a more ambitious form by editing one generated by a Form Wizard.

The first form is a telephone list for our Contacts.

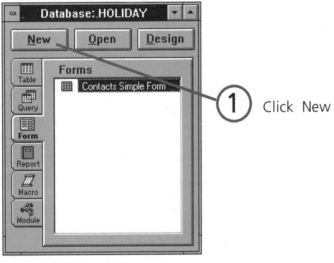

① Click New

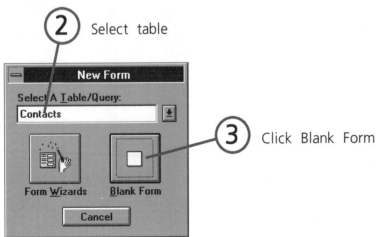

② Select table

③ Click Blank Form

Basic steps

1 From the **Form** tab in the **Database** window, click the **New Form** icon

Or

1 click [**New**]

2 At the **New Form** dialog box, drop down the list of **Tables/Queries** and choose the Table or Query (*Contacts* in our case) to design your form around

3 Click **Blank Form**

❑ You arrive at the Form Design screen.

> ## Take note
>
> **You can use the tools or the View menu options to change views and switch screen elements on or off.**
>
> **If your Toolbox or Field List are not displayed, open them now.**

108

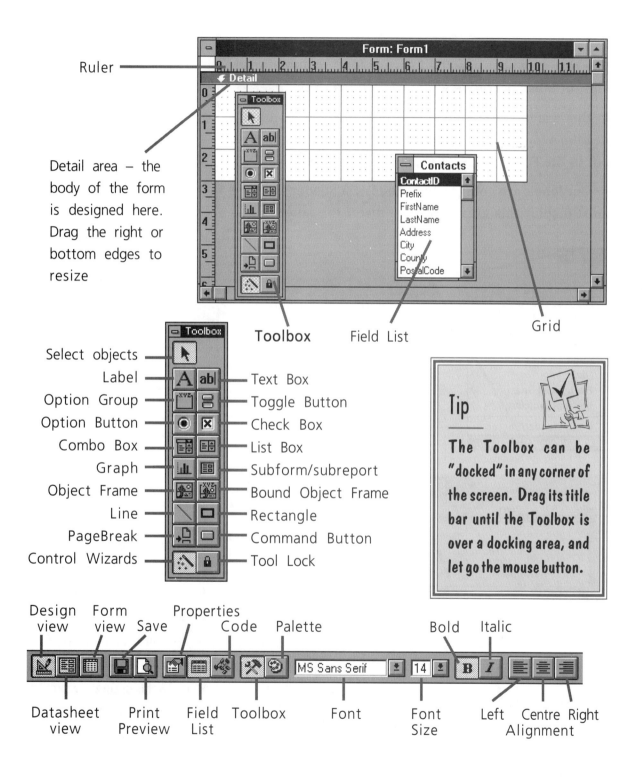

Ruler

Detail area – the body of the form is designed here. Drag the right or bottom edges to resize

Form: Form1

◆ Detail

Toolbox

Contacts

ContactID
Prefix
FirstName
LastName
Address
City
County
PostalCode

Toolbox   Field List   Grid

Select objects
Label — Text Box
Option Group — Toggle Button
Option Button — Check Box
Combo Box — List Box
Graph — Subform/subreport
Object Frame — Bound Object Frame
Line — Rectangle
PageBreak — Command Button
Control Wizards — Tool Lock

Toolbox

Tip

The Toolbox can be "docked" in any corner of the screen. Drag its title bar until the Toolbox is over a docking area, and let go the mouse button.

Design view   Form view   Save   Properties   Code   Palette   Bold   Italic

MS Sans Serif   14   **B** *I*

Datasheet view   Print Preview   Field List   Toolbox   Font   Font Size   Left   Centre   Right
Alignment

Headers and footers

Usually, you will have some descriptive text in your form. The text may be a heading for your form, column headings, or some narrative with instructions to the user.

In this example we want the form title and the column headings for our tabular layout. This text, which we will put in the Form header area, is called a **Label**.

As our labels are going to be in the Form header area, we must display this area first, then insert the labels.

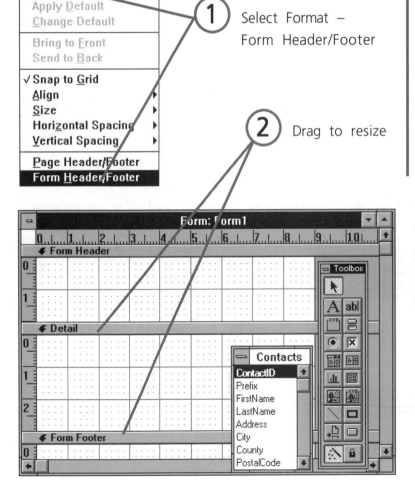

Select Format –
Form Header/Footer

Drag to resize

1 Open the **Format** menu and choose **Form Header/Footer**

❑ A Form Header area appears above, and a Form Footer area appears below, the Detail area

2 Resize the Header and Footer areas as necessary by dragging the lower edge of the area, up or down (we need to increase the size of the Header and decrease the size of the footer - in fact make it disappear!)

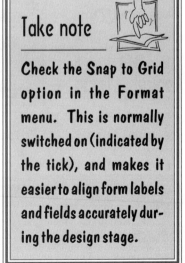

Take note

Check the Snap to Grid option in the Format menu. This is normally switched on (indicated by the tick), and makes it easier to align form labels and fields accurately during the design stage.

Basic steps

Adding Labels

1 Click the **Label** tool

2 Move the mouse pointer – now $+_A$ – to where you want your first label

3 Click and drag to draw a rectangle

4 Type in your label text eg *TELEPHONE LIST*

5 Repeat steps 1-4 for each column heading ie *NAME, HOME PHONE NO* and *WORK PHONE NO*

The headings we are going to put on our form are purely descriptive – they are not part of the table the form is designed around. We can therefore make the text anything we want. This can be very useful for instructions .

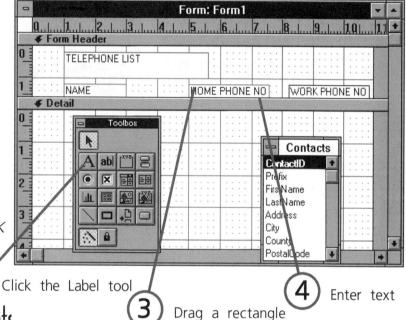

① Click the Label tool

③ Drag a rectangle

④ Enter text

Adjusting Design Elements

If you position a label (or any element) incorrectly or make it too big or small, this is easily amended. First select it by clicking anywhere on it. Note the handles that appear around the edges of a selected element.

To Resize

1 Point to a handle. The pointer changes to a double headed arrow

2 Drag the arrow to resize

To Move

1 Point to an edge (not a handle). The pointer changes to a hand

2 Drag the element into position

To Delete

1 Press the **[Delete]** key

Formatting the labels

Now that your labels are on your form, in the correct postion and the correct size, you might want to enhance the appearance of them so they stand out clearly as headings. You might want to make them bigger, or bolder, or in italics - you choose!

Select the label

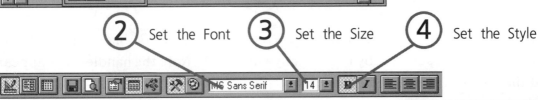

② Set the Font ③ Set the Size ④ Set the Style

Take note

You may have to resize labels if a larger font size results in an overspill!

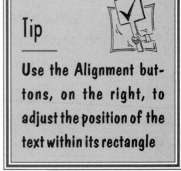

Tip

Use the Alignment buttons, on the right, to adjust the position of the text within its rectangle

112

Basic steps

1 Click [■] to display the **Field List**

2 Drag a field from the list (*Lastname*), and drop it in the Detail area

❑ *Both* components of the field are selected, but we want to deal with them separately

3 Click on the **field name** section to select it, and press **[Delete]**

4 If necessary, reposition and/or resize the field detail component

5 Repeat steps 2-4 for each field (*Prefix*, *Homephone* and *Workphone*) you require

❑ Once all the fields are in place, you may need to reduce the depth of the detail area, to produce a neat list in Form view. (See page 115)

We now need to position the fields we require in the Detail area of the form. This is done by simply clicking and dragging the required field from the field list to its destination on the form. When a field is dragged over however, it has two components - one for the field name and one for the field detail.

As we are describing the information that will be displayed in the Detail area in our column headings, we do not require the field name section.

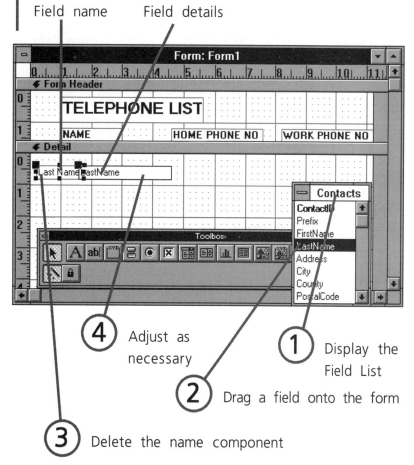

Field name   Field details

④ Adjust as necessary

① Display the Field List

② Drag a field onto the form

③ Delete the name component

6

Save your form

Obviously, you need to save your form design if you want to keep it. You can save your design at any time, you don't need to wait until you have set the whole thing up. If you are designing a complex form, save it regularly.

Save Form and Save Form As ...

If you have already saved your form, and have edited the design since the last save, you can use **File - Save Form** (or click) to replace the old version of the form with the new one.

If you want to save the edited version as a separate form, you must use **File - Save Form As** to give it a different name. This can be very useful if you are designing several similar forms – once the first one is saved, you can edit it to produce the next then save it with a different name.

Take note

If a form has never been saved, whichever Save you use will take you to the Save As dialog box

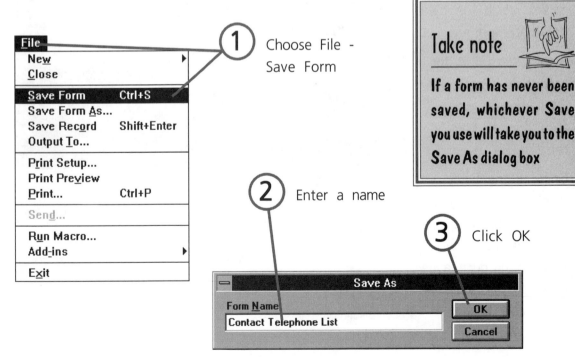

Choose File - Save Form

Enter a name

Click OK

114

Basic steps

1 Click the **Form View**
icon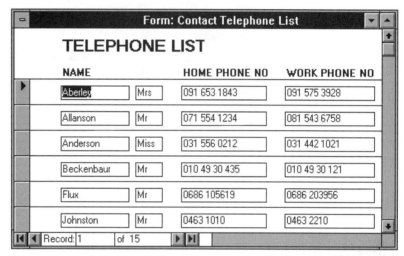

❏ The Form is displayed
in Form view

2 Position the insertion
point anywhere in the
LastName field and
click the Sort, Ascend-
ing icon to sort
the list into alphabeti-
cal order

❏ You can print
the form directly, or
preview it before
printing

3 Double click the control menu box to close
the form.

Take note

If you are not happy with the
look of the form, click the Design icon to go back to Design
view and edit it (remember to
save any changes you make).

Form view

Let us look at our form in Form view, where the headings
describe the form contents, and the record details are
picked up from the table and repeated as many times as
will fit on the paper or screen. We will **sort** the records
listed in ascending order on *LastName*, as this will make
the form view easier to use.

It is assumed you are in the Form Design screen.

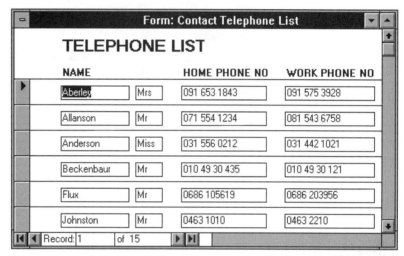

Form: Contact Telephone List

TELEPHONE LIST

NAME		HOME PHONE NO	WORK PHONE NO
Aberley	Mrs	091 653 1843	091 575 3928
Allanson	Mr	071 554 1234	081 543 6758
Anderson	Miss	031 556 0212	031 442 1021
Beckenbaur	Mr	010 49 30 435	010 49 30 121
Flux	Mr	0686 105619	0686 203956
Johnston	Mr	0463 1010	0463 2210

Record: 1 of 15

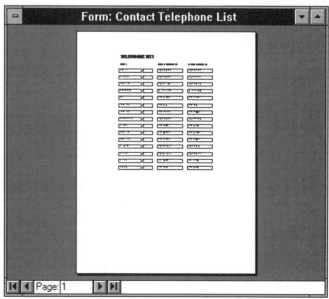

Form: Contact Telephone List

Page: 1

Using Form Wizard

There are several Wizards to help you design your forms.
We will build a simple form using one of the Wizards, then
explore some more form design features to customise it.
We will base this form on the *Accommodation* table.

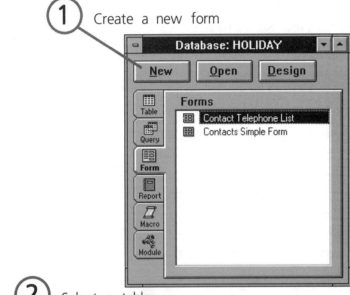

① Create a new form

② Select a table

③ Click Forn Wizards

④ Choose a Wizard

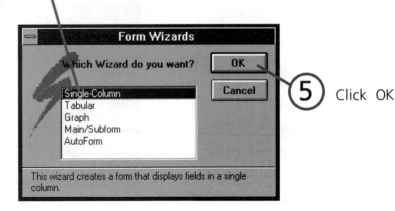

⑤ Click OK

1 From the **Form** tab in
the Database window,
choose **New**, or
click the **New Form**
icon

2 At the **New Form**
prompt, choose *Ac-
commodation* from
the **Tables/Queries** list

3 Click **Form Wizards**

4 There are 5 Wizards to
choose from. Choose
the **Single Column
Wizard** for this form.

❑ This creates a simple
form (like that gener-
ated by Autoform in
Section 5).

5 Click **OK**

Basic steps

1 Add the desired fields from the **Available fields:** list, in the right order, to the **Field Order on Form** list

2 Click **Next >**

3 Choose the **Style** of form you want -try **Standard** for now.

4 Click **Next >**

Take note

A sample of the currently selected Style option is shown at the top left

Setting up the form

The Wizard will need to be told what fields to include, what style to use and what title to write in the header, but once it has that, it can take care of the rest.

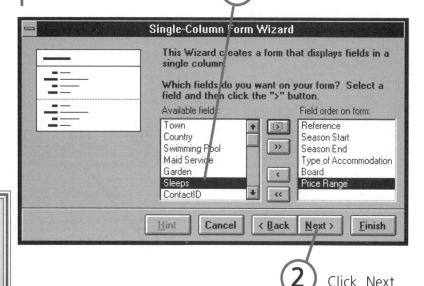

① Add fields to the list

② Click Next

③ Choose a style

④ Click Next

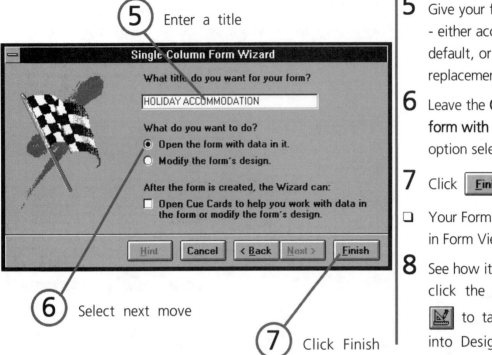

⑤ Enter a title

⑥ Select next move

⑦ Click Finish

5 Give your form a title
- either accept the
default, or type in a
replacement

6 Leave the **Open the
form with data in it**
option selected

7 Click [Finish]

❑ Your Form is displayed
in Form View

8 See how it looks, then
click the **Design** icon
to take your form
into Design view.

⑧ Check the design to see
what style or layout
changes you want to make

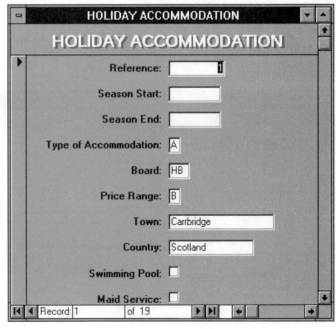

Basic steps

Editing the design

❑ **To select multiple fields**

1 Click on the first field you want to select

2 Hold the **[Shift]** key down, and click on the next field

3 Continue to [Shift]-click until you have selected all the fields

❑ You can now move, resize, delete or format the selected fields

4 To deselect the fields, simply click on another area of the form

Once the fields are in the form, you can adjust them as appropriate. You can move and resize the fields as you did when setting up the Telephone List form.

There may be times when you get a group of fields in the desired position relative to each other, but you want to move them up, down, right or left a bit on your form. You can drag each field, one at a time, but it's easier (and quicker) to select all the fields, and move them in one go. Likewise, if you want to give the same font or style to a group of elements, it is simplest to do them together.

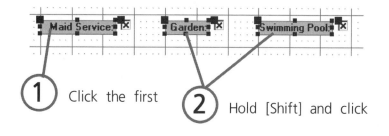

① Click the first ② Hold [Shift] and click

The form after adjusting the layout

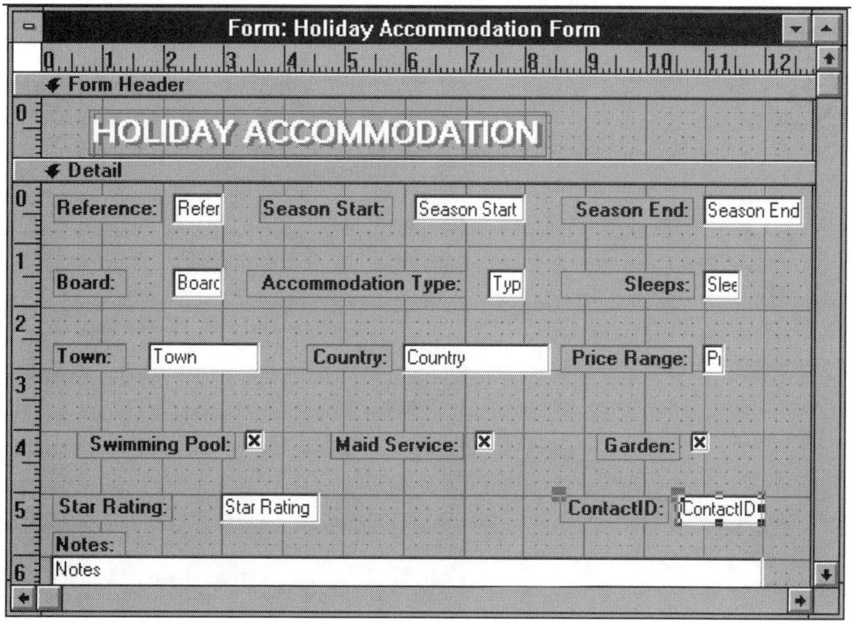

Tip

If you have not saved your form, do so now!

The form after adjusting the layout window showing "Form: Holiday Accommodation Form" with HOLIDAY ACCOMMODATION header and fields: Reference, Season Start, Season End, Board, Accommodation Type, Sleeps, Town, Country, Price Range, Swimming Pool, Maid Service, Garden, Star Rating, ContactID, Notes.

Combo boxes

The Combo box is something that you are well accustomed to as a Windows user. Fields in dialog boxes and on toolbars, where you drop down a list of alternatives (like the Font or Size tool) are Combo boxes. We will use them for the *Board*, *Type of Accommodation* and *Price Range* fields. Users can then select an option from the list.

1 Take you form into Design view

2 Delete the *Board* field

3 Check that the **Control Wizard** tool is ON

4 Click the **Combo box** tool

5 Drag the *Board* field from the field list onto your form

6 At the **Combo Box Wizard** dialog box, select I **will type in the values ...**

7 How many columns?

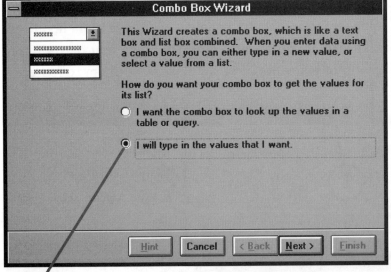

6 Select I will type..

9 Set the width

8 Type in values

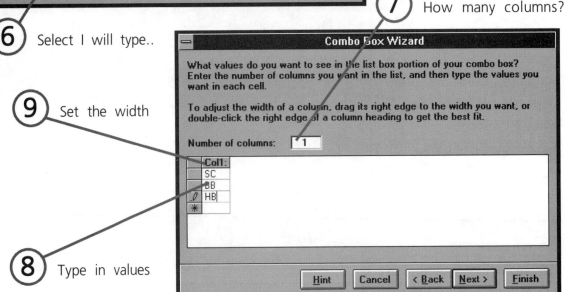

120

7 Specify the number of columns in your Combo box - one for this example

8 Enter the values for the Combo box list - *SC*, *BB* and *HB*

9 Set the column width

10 Select the field to store the Combo box value in (*Board* in our example)

11 Give your Combo box a label - either accept the default or enter your own

12 Click **Finish** and you are returned to Form Design view, with the Combo Box in place.

❑ Use the same steps to create a Combo box for the *Type of Accommodation* field. The entries in the list would be C, A, F and R (for Cottage, Apartment, Flat and Room).

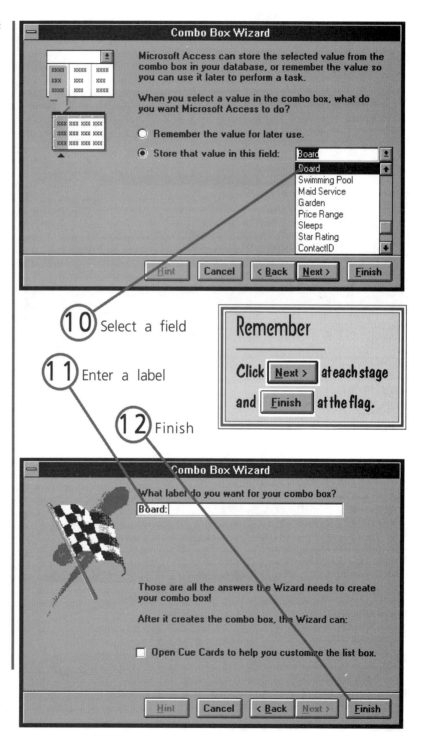

(10) Select a field

(11) Enter a label

(12) Finish

Remember

Click **Next >** at each stage and **Finish** at the flag.

Look up values

With the Price Range field, we will look up the values in the Price table, rather than key them in.

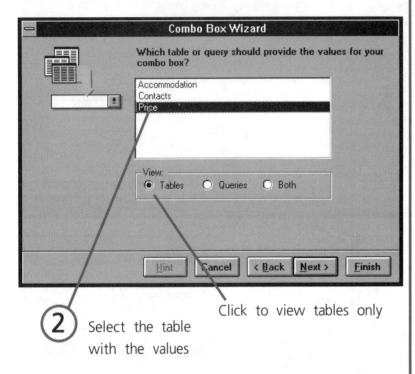

Click to view tables only

2 Select the table with the values

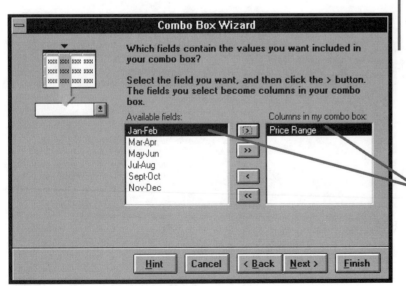

3 Add the field to the list

1 Follow steps 1-6 above, but using the *Price Range* field and at the **Combo Box Wizard** dialog box, select **I want the combo box to look up the values...**

2 Choose the Table or Query the values are in (*Price*) - you can list just either the Tables, Queries or both from your Database by selecting a **View** option

3 Add the field that contains the values to the **Columns in my combo box** list (*Price Range*)

4 Set the Column Width

5 Complete the Wizard as per steps 10-12 on page 121

6 Click the **Form View** icon 📰 to take you through into Form view.

Your form should now look something like this. When you click the drop down button to the right of your Combo boxes, the list of options will drop down so you can choose the one required.

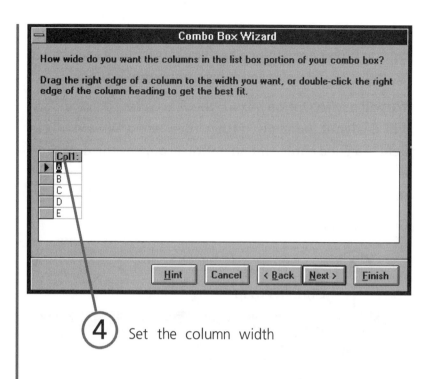

④ Set the column width

Click to drop the list down

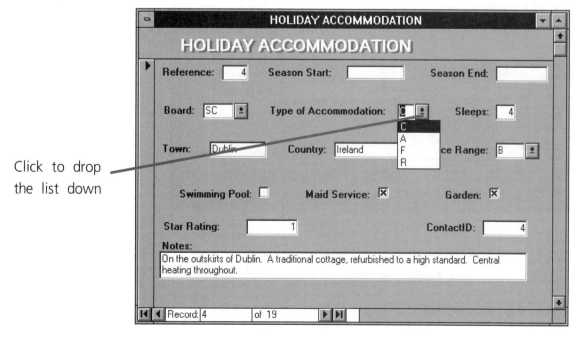

Option boxes

Another way of displaying data is to use an Option box. Option boxes are useful when you have a limited number of options, and you can choose only one of them.

We will use an Option box for the *Star Rating* field, and we will design it manually, rather than use a Wizard. This field is a good choice for an option group, as the data type is Number, and its values are *1, 2, 3* or *4*. Access will set the Option property value to 1, 2, 3 and 4 automatically.

Go back into Design view.

1 Switch off the Control Wizards

2 Delete the *Star-Rating* field

3 Click the **Option group** tool

4 Click on your form to place the Option group and resize it as necessary

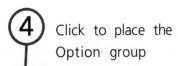 Click to place the Option group

Resize to give room for 4 buttons

Option group label – this will need changing

124

Basic steps

1 Select the Button tool

2 Switch on the **Tool Lock** 🔒

3 Click in 4 places within the Option group

4 Switch the **Lock** off

5 Select the Pointer ▶ (this has the effect of switching off the Button tool)

Take note

The Option Group and Button labels need to be changed to something more meaningful. The Group label could become *Star-Rating*; the Button labels *1-Star, 2-Star, 3-Star* and *4-Star*. To edit a label, click to select the field, double click to select the label, then retype it.

Placing buttons

We are now going to add 4 buttons to the Option group - one for each star rating. A tool will normally only let you place one copy of an element at each selection, but there is a way to keep it active. Instead of having to select the Button tool for each option, you can **lock** onto it with the **Tool Lock**.

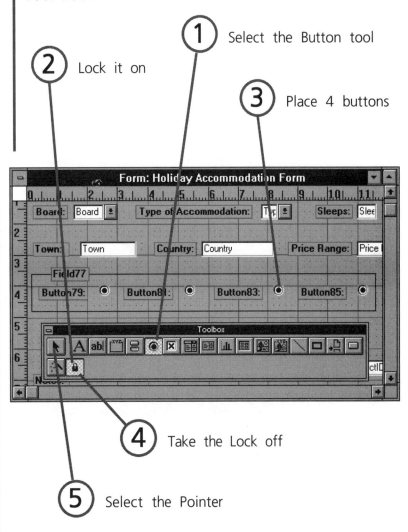

① Select the Button tool

② Lock it on

③ Place 4 buttons

④ Take the Lock off

⑤ Select the Pointer

Control Source

We must now tell Access where to find the information for this Option group, and where to store the values. This is done in the **Data Properties** dialog box for the group

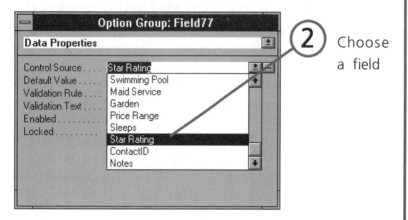

Choose a field

Final Touches

Give the Option Group a sunken appearance, to make it stand out as a group on the form.

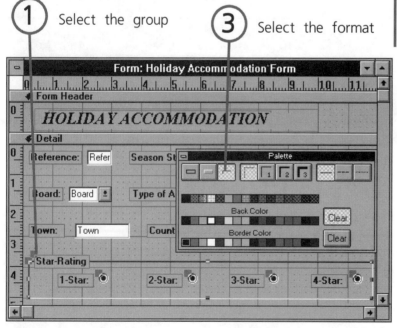

① Select the group

③ Select the format

❑ **Control Source**

1 Select the Option group and click the **Properties** tool 📇 to open the **Data Properties** dialog box

2 For the **Control Source**, choose the Star Rating field

3 Close the Data Properties dialog box

❑ **Final touches**

1 Select the Option Group

2 Click the Palette tool 🎨 to open the Palette

3 Click the Sunken Appearance tool ⌐

4 Close the Palette

5 Save the design, and click the Form view icon 🏢 to go into Form view.

Basic steps

1 Take the form into Design view if necessary

2 Open the **Edit** menu and choose **Tab Order**

3 Click [**Auto Order**] to have Access rearrange the tab order to correspond to the field order on the form, from left to right and top to bottom

4 Click **OK**

Since Form Wizard built your form, you have moved several fields around. When you press **[Tab]** to move through it in Form view, you will find that you appear to jump all over the place, in apparently no sensible order. Access sets up the tab order for the fields in the order in which they were defined when the form was originally set up. The tab order can easily be edited if required.

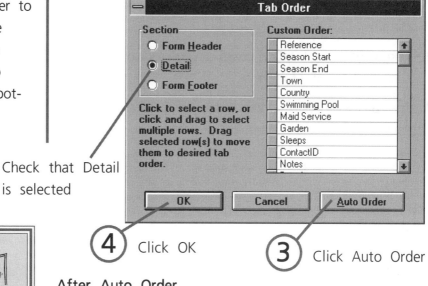

Check that Detail is selected

④ Click OK

③ Click Auto Order

After Auto Order

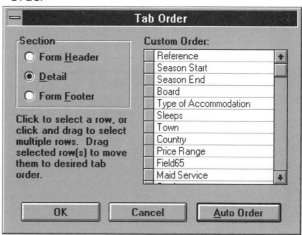

Take note

To move a field individually, in the Tab Order dialog box, select the field you want to move (click its selector button), then drag the selector button to move the selected row to its new position.

Summary

❏ **Forms** allow you to customise your input and viewing screens

❏ Your **fields** can be placed anywhere on your form

❏ **Text** (for instructions and/or labels) can be included on your form to enhance its appearance, and make it easier to use

❏ Forms can be designed from scratch, or you can use one of the **Form Wizards** to help you design your form

❏ **Combo boxes** and **Option boxes** can be used to simplify data entry to forms

❏ The **Palette** can be used to put the final touches to your form

10 Reports

The Report design screen

Reports provide the most effective way of creating a printed copy of data extracted or calculated from the tables and queries in your database. They might be invoices, purchase orders, presentation materials or mailing labels.

Many of the features used in forms design are also used in report design. There are also a number of features that are unique to the Report environment. We will build our first report from scratch, and base it on the *Accommodation* table.

Basic steps

1   Click **New** on the **Report** tab in the Database window or the **New Report** icon

2   At the **New Report** dialog box, choose the table on to base your report

3   Click **Blank Report**

❑   The blank report screen opens, with the Toolbox and Field List

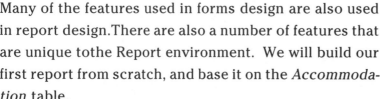

Click New

Select a table

Click Blank Report

Report Design screen

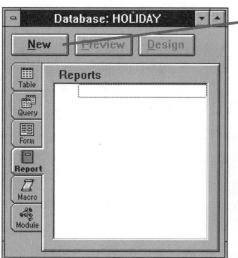

Basic steps

Setting up the Page Header and Detail area

1 Use the **Label** tool ![A] to insert a field for the Page Header

2 Key in a suitable header eg *"LIST OF ACCOMMODATION BY STAR-RATING"*

3 Select the header and format it

4 Click the **Line** tool ![line], lock it on, then click and drag the lines above and below the header.

5 Click the Pointer tool and select both lines

6 Open the Palette with the **Palette** tool ![palette]

7 Select the 3pt line

8 Drag the lower edge of the **Detail** area up to give a sensible row height for our list

9 Drag the required fields (eg *Country*, *Town*, *Board*, *Sleeps* and *Price*) into place on your report

The techniques used here are very similar to those used in Forms design at this stage.

② Key in a header

③ Format it

④ Draw two lines

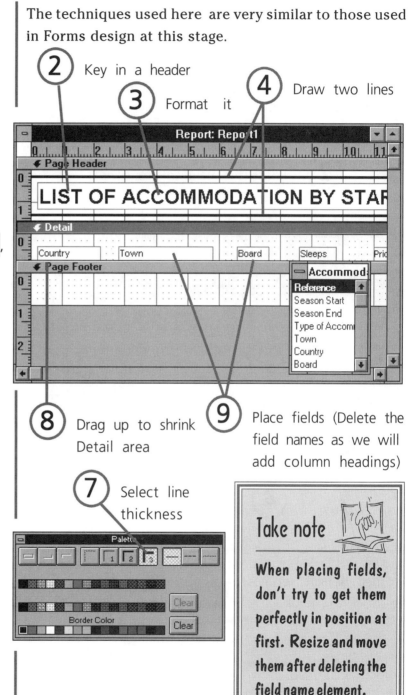

⑧ Drag up to shrink Detail area

⑨ Place fields (Delete the field names as we will add column headings)

⑦ Select line thickness

> ## Take note
>
> When placing fields, don't try to get them perfectly in position at first. Resize and move them after deleting the field name element.

Grouping records

The records in our report are going to be grouped, so all the accommodation with a 1-star rating is together, all that with a 2-star rating is together and so on.

The Sorting and Grouping icon on the Toolbar is used to group your records.

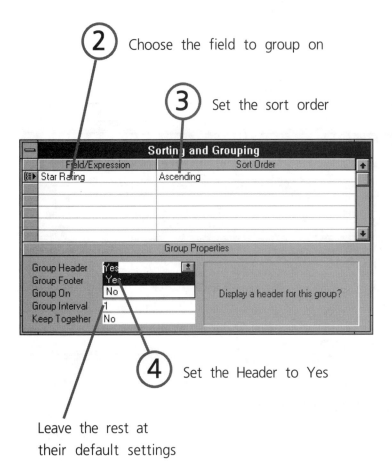

② Choose the field to group on

③ Set the sort order

Set the Header to Yes

Leave the rest at their default settings

1 Click the **Sorting and Grouping** tool

2 In the **Field/Expression** column, choose the **Star Rating** field from the list (this is the field on which we are going to group our records)

3 The **Sort Order** should be **Ascending** - to give 1-star to 4-star

4 Set the **Group Header** field to **Yes** - this will display a header area for our group

5 Close the Sorting and Grouping dialog box

Take note

The Sorting and Grouping tool is a toggle - you can use it to open and close the Sorting and Grouping dialog box.

Basic steps

1 Click and drag the *Star Rating* field over into the **Star Rating Header** area

2 Format the name and detail area of the field as required eg bold, larger font size, etc

3 Use the Label tool [A] to set up the column headings; key in the column headings required and format as you wish

Designing the Group Header area

We are going to have our grouped records preceded by a heading in the header area:- *Star-Rating 1*, *Star-Rating 2*, *Star-Rating 3*, *Star-Rating 4*

In addition to the group heading, we will put the column headings for the detail in here too.

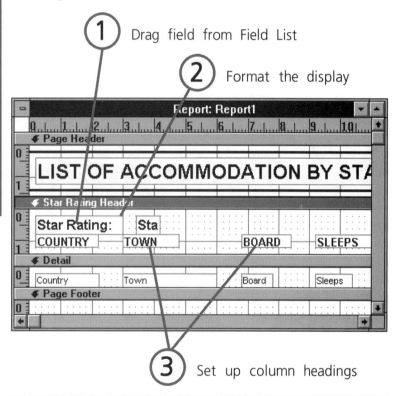

① Drag field from Field List

② Format the display

③ Set up column headings

Sorting grouped records

We now want to specify how we want our records sorted within each *Star Rating* group. In this example, the main sort field within the group will be *Country*, and then *Town*. We must therefore tell Access to group our fields by *Star Rating*, and sort that field into Ascending order. Within each group, the records have to be sorted into ascending order based on *Country*, and within each Country, the records have to be sorted into ascending order on *Town*.

1 Click the **Sorting and Grouping** tool to open the Sorting and Grouping dialog box

2 In the second row, choose *Country* in the **Field/Expression** column, and **Ascending** as the **Sort order**

3 In the third row, choose *Town* in the **Field/Expression** column, and **Ascending** as the **Sort order**

4 Close the Sorting and Grouping dialog box

② Select field and set sort order

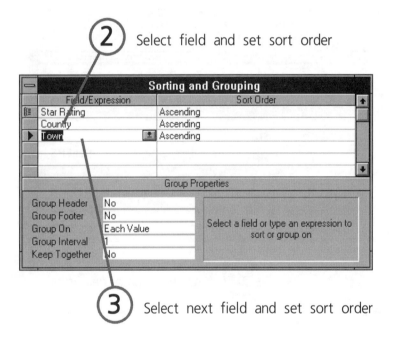

③ Select next field and set sort order

134

Basic steps

1 Click the **Text Box** tool, **ab** then click in the **Page Footer** area to place the Text Box

2 Delete the Field name and reposition the detail section if necessary

3 Select the detail section

4 Click the **Properties** tool 🖼 to open the **Properties** dialog box

5 In the **Control Source** field key in *=Now()* This expression returns the current date and time from your system

6 Close the Properties dialog box

7 Left align 📄 the Text Box so it lines up at the left margin of your report (the data will align to the right by default)

Adding a text box

We are now ready to design the Footer area of our report. We will insert an Text Box here, where we can display the date and time of producing the report.

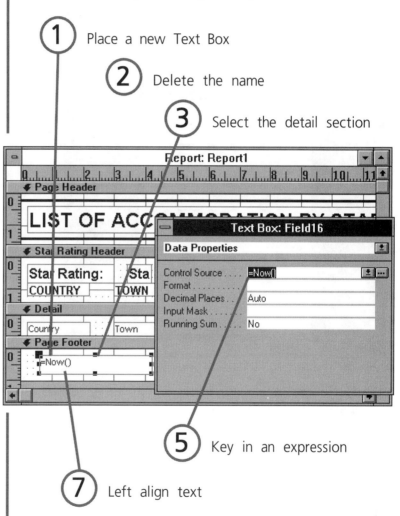

1 Place a new Text Box

2 Delete the name

3 Select the detail section

5 Key in an expression

7 Left align text

Preview and print

You can now Print Preview your report, and print out a hard copy if you wish. There are two Preview choices here. The **Sample Preview** will give you a quick preview using sample data; the **Print Preview** takes longer to produce, but gives you a preview of the whole report.

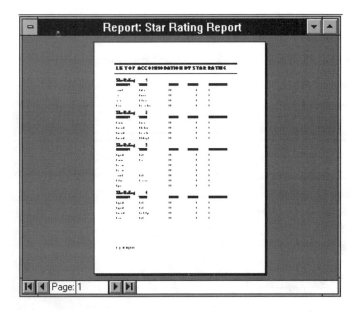

Basic steps

1 Click the icon for **Print Preview** or **Sample Preview**

2 Print the report if you wish

3 Close the **Print Preview** window

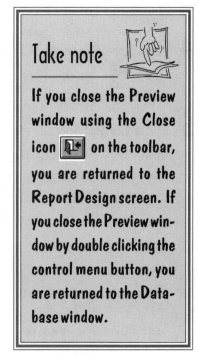

Take note

If you close the Preview window using the Close icon on the toolbar, you are returned to the Report Design screen. If you close the Preview window by double clicking the control menu button, you are returned to the Database window.

Tip

Don't forget to save the report if you want to keep it for future use. Click the Save icon  and give your report a name.

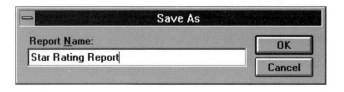

Mailing labels

1 Click **New** on the
Report tab on the
Database window, or
click the New Report
icon 🔲

2 Choose the table on
which you wish to
base your mailing
labels (*Contacts*)

3 Click **Report Wizards**

4 Choose the Report
Wizard you want to
use (**Mailing Label**)

5 Click **OK**

This time, we will create a report to print Mailing Labels.
We will use a Report Wizard, to take us through the steps
required to generate them.

The mailing labels are for the owners we have for each
property in our database. The name and address details
required for the labels are in our Contacts table.

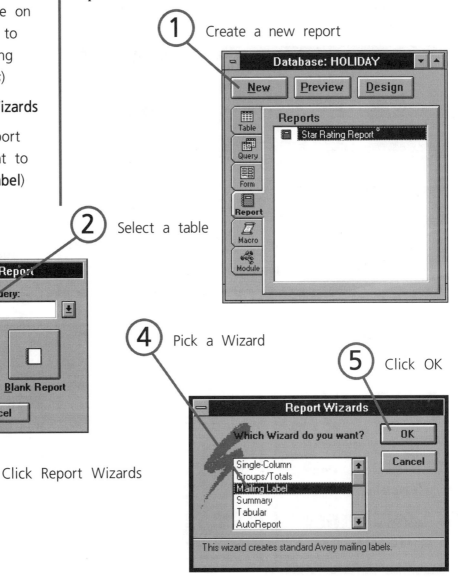

① Create a new report

② Select a table

③ Click Report Wizards

④ Pick a Wizard

⑤ Click OK

Specifying the Label Design

The next stage is to specify the layout. Getting data to fit comfortably on labels can be a tricky business, so check how they will look – and edit the design if necessary – before you print.

① Add fields, with separators as needed

The dots show spaces inserted between fields

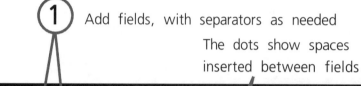

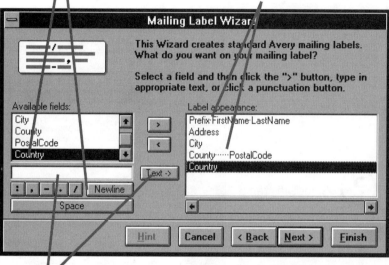

② Type text then add to label

③ Specify sort field

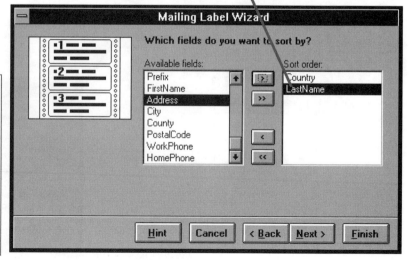

Tip

Remember to click Next > when you have done at each stage.

138

5 Choose the appropriate label code, and
the **Label Type**

6 Modify the font style,
size, attributes and
colour as required

7 Choose **See the mailing labels as they will
look printed**

8 Click **Finish**

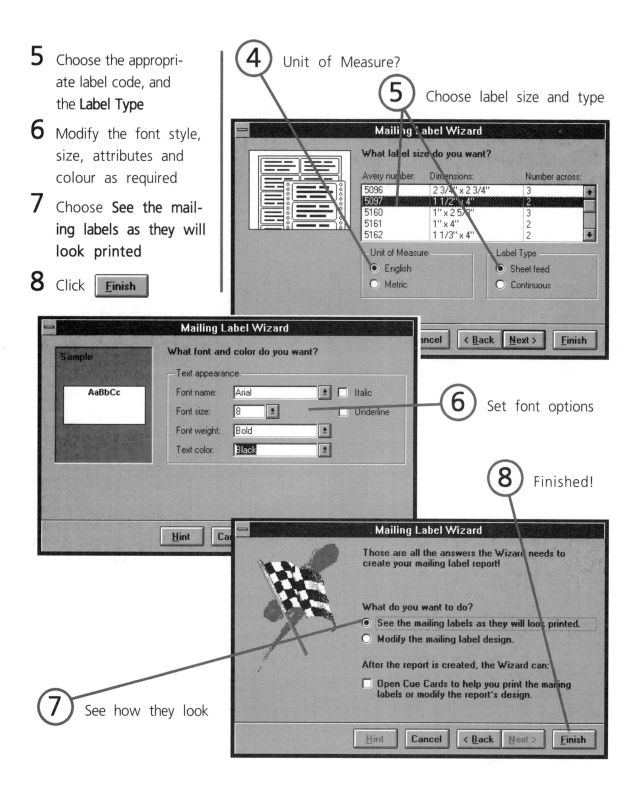

④ Unit of Measure?

⑤ Choose label size and type

Mailing Label Wizard

What label size do you want?

Avery number:	Dimensions:	Number across:
5096	2 3/4" x 2 3/4"	3
5097	1 1/2" x 4"	2
5160	1" x 2 5/8"	3
5161	1" x 4"	2
5162	1 1/3" x 4"	2

Unit of Measure
● English
○ Metric

Label Type
● Sheet feed
○ Continuous

Cancel   < Back   Next >   Finish

Mailing Label Wizard

What font and color do you want?

Sample

AaBbCc

Text appearance

Font name: Arial   ▼   ☐ Italic

Font size: 8 ▼   ☐ Underline

Font weight: Bold   ▼

Text color: Black   ▼

⑥ Set font options

⑧ Finished!

Hint   Ca

Mailing Label Wizard

Those are all the answers the Wizard needs to
create your mailing label report!

What do you want to do?
● See the mailing labels as they will look printed.
○ Modify the mailing label design.

After the report is created, the Wizard can:
☐ Open Cue Cards to help you print the mailing
labels or modify the report's design.

⑦ See how they look

Hint   Cancel   < Back   Next >   Finish

Editing the Design

The labels are displayed in Print Preview. You can use the Print Setup to modify margins and orientation if necessary, or click the Print icon to print your labels out.

If you want to modify the design of your labels, or save the label report for future use, you must return to Design view by clicking the Close icon on the Print Preview toolbar.

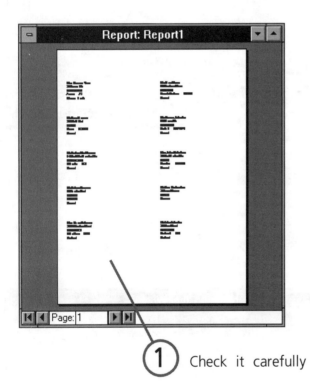

(1) Check it carefully

The Print Preview here shows us that we could have used a larger font without running out of space.

Basic steps

1 Check the **Print Preview** to see what needs to be done

2 Close the **Print Preview** screen with the Close icon

❏ You are returned to the **Design** screen for the Mailing Labels

3 Use any of the Design features available to modify the design of your label

4 Click the **Save** icon to Save the label design

5 Give the report a suitable name

6 Click **OK**

7 Click the Print icon 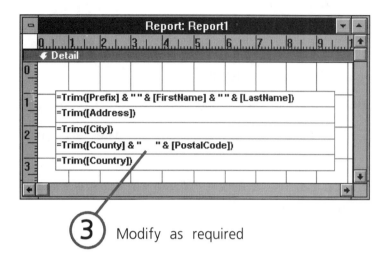 to print the labels if required

8 Close the Report

❑ You are returned to the **Report** tab in the **Database** window. Your new report should be listed.

Report: Report1

◀ Detail

=Trim([Prefix] & " " & [FirstName] & " " & [LastName])
=Trim([Address])
=Trim([City])
=Trim([County] & "   " & [PostalCode])
=Trim([Country])

(3) Modify as required

(5) Enter a name

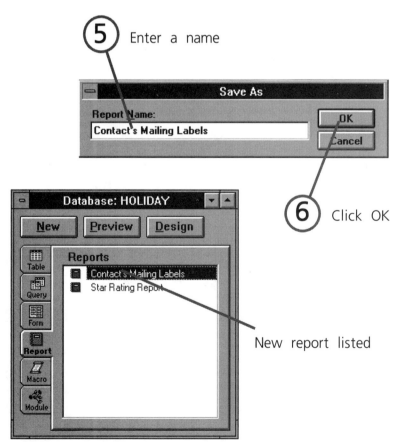

Save As

Report Name:

Contact's Mailing Labels

OK

Cancel

(6) Click OK

Database: HOLIDAY

New | Preview | Design

Table
Query
Form
Report
Macro
Module

Reports

Contact's Mailing Labels
Star Rating Report

New report listed

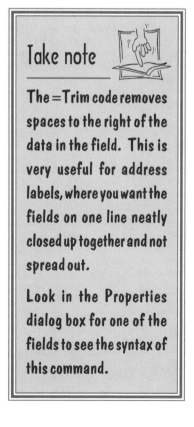

Take note

The =Trim code removes spaces to the right of the data in the field. This is very useful for address labels, where you want the fields on one line neatly closed up together and not spread out.

Look in the Properties dialog box for one of the fields to see the syntax of this command.

Summary

❑ Reports provide an effective way of presenting data extracted or calculated from your queries and tables

❑ Many of the **Forms design techniques** are also used in Report design

❑ Records can be **grouped and sorted** in your reports

❑ **Text Boxes** can be used to insert dates and times into your report

❑ You can use a **Report Wizard** to simplify the printing of Mailing Labels

Appendices

A Accommodation table

Ref	Season Start	Season End	Type of Accomm.	Country	Board	Swimming Pool	Maid Service	Garden	Price Range	Sleeps	Contact ID
1			A	Scotland	HB	No	No	Yes	B	4	1
2			F	England	SC	No	Yes	No	C	4	2
3	01/02/95	01/12/95	R	Wales	BB	No	Yes	No	C	2	3
4			C	Ireland	SC	No	Yes	Yes	B	4	4
5	18/01/95	10/12/95	F	Scotland	SC	Yes	Yes	No	D	6	5
6			C	France	SC	No	Yes	Yes	A	4	6
7			R	Germany	HB	No	Yes	Yes	A	2	7
8			C	Germany	SC	No	Yes	Yes	B	4	7
9			C	France	SC	No	Yes	Yes	C	6	6
10			A	Scotland	HB	Yes	Yes	No	D	4	8
11			F	England	SC	Yes	Yes	No	D	4	9
12			A	Wales	BB	Yes	No	Yes	E	4	3
13			F	Scotland	SC	No	Yes	No	E	4	1
14			C	Italy	SC	Yes	Yes	Yes	C	6	10
15			A	Spain	SC	Yes	Yes	No	D	4	11
16			C	England	SC	No	Yes	Yes	C	2	2
17			R	France	BB	No	Yes	Yes	C	4	12
18			C	Orkney	SC	No	Yes	Yes	B	4	1
19			A	Jersey	SC	Yes	Yes	Yes	C	4	13
20			R	Ireland	HB	Yes	Yes	Yes	D	2	14

ContactID	Prefix	FirstName	LastName	Address	City	County	Postal Code	Country	Work Phone	Home Phone
1	Mr	John	Johnston	24 Main Street	INVERNESS	Highland	IV10	Scotland	0463 2210	0463 1010
2	Miss	Elaine	Anderson	22 St Stephen Street	EDINBURGH	Midlothian	EH10	Scotland	031 442 1021	031 556 0212
3	Mrs	Elizabeth	Watson	14 Mill Wynd West	GLASGOW	Strathclyde	G13	Scotland	041 665 1043	041 510 5103
4	Mr	Gordon	McPherson	14 Worthington Way	BIRMINGHAM	Midlands	B24	England	021 557 9321	021 676 1999
5	Mr	Hanz	Beckenbaur	24 Lang Strasse	BERLIN			Germany	010 49 30 121	010 49 30 435
6	Mr	Andrew	Simpson	10 Dolphin Road	LONDON		N18 2WS	England	081 475 1010	071 442 4102
7	Mrs	Alice	Aberley	St Stephens Manse	PETERLEE	Co Durham	SR8 5AJ	England	091 575 3928	091 653 1843
8	Mr	Brian	Allanson	328 Bath Road	ILFORD	Essex	1G2 6PN	England	081 543 6758	071 544 1234
9	Mrs	Pamela	Johnston	10 Wilson Way	DEREFORD	Norfolk	NR19 1JG	England	0362 331112	0362 574098
10	Miss	Joan	Robertson	24 West Linton Way	KENDAL	Cumbria	LA9 6EH	England	0539 561732	0539 665577
11	Mr	William	Flux	132 London Road	CARNO	Montgomery	SY17 5LU	Wales	0686 203956	0686 105619
12	Miss	Amanda	Wilson	14 High Way	LAMPETER	Dyfed	SA4 8NW	Wales	0570 30651	0570 61234
13	Mr	William	Robertson	Hill View Rise	STROMNESS	Orkney	OK10	Scotland	0856 103212	0856 114322
14	Miss	Suzanne	Young	24 Causeway St	CLEMENT	Jersey	J21	Channel Is	0534 14261	0534 66310
15	Mr	Paul	Mitchell	45 Hill Top View	ABERDEEN	Aberdeenshire	AB24	Scotland	0224 10231	0224 54123

C Price table

Price Range	Jan-Feb	Mar-Apr	May-Jun	Jul-Aug	Sep-Oct	Nov-Dec
A	£240	£260	£300	£350	£310	£260
B	£260	£280	£320	£380	£320	£280
C	£275	£296	£340	£310	£360	£300
D	£285	£310	£370	£420	£390	£350
E	£300	£340	£410	£470	£425	£395

Index